DATE DUE

PHILOSOPHICAL & CULTURAL VALUES:

APPLYING ETHICS IN SCHOOLS

George Crawford
Janice Nicklaus

EYE ON EDUCATION
6 DEPOT WAY WEST, SUITE 106
LARCHMONT, NY 10538
(914) 833–0551
(914) 833–0761 fax

Library of Congress Cataloging-in-Publication Data

Crawford, George, 1937–
    Philosophical and cultural values : applying ethics in schools / by George Crawford and Janice Nicklaus.
        p. cm.
    Includes bibliographical references.
    ISBN 1-883001-82-X
    1. School principals—Professional ethics—United States. 2. Educational leadership—Moral and ethical aspects—United States. I. Nicklaus, Janice, 1949– II. Title.

    LB2831.92.C72 2000
    371.2'012–dc21

                                                                    99-047167

10 9 8 7 6 5 4 3 2 1

Editorial and production services provided by
Richard H. Adin Freelance Editorial Services,
52 Oakwood Blvd., Poughkeepsie, NY 12603
(914-471-3566)

The School Leadership Library

David A. Erlandson and
Alfred P. Wilson, General Editors

The School Leadership Library, a series of 21 books, shows you what successful principals and other school leaders must know and be able to do. Grounded in best knowledge and practice, these books demonstrate best practices of effective principals. They provide recommendations which can be applied to a school leader's daily work.

Each volume includes practical materials, such as:

+ checklists
+ sample letters and memos
+ model forms
+ action plans

What should an effective principal know and be able to do? Members of the National Policy Board for Educational Administration (sponsored by NAESP, NASSP, AASA, ASCD, NCPEA, UCEA, and other professional organizations) developed a set of 21 "domains," or building blocks, that represent the essential knowledge and skills of successful principals. Each volume in this series is dedicated to explaining and applying one of these building blocks.

Contact Eye On Education for more details.

The School Leadership Library

The Functional Domains

Leadership Gary M. Crow, L. Joseph Matthews, and Lloyd E. Mccleary

Information Collection Short, Short, and Brinson, Jnr.

Problem Analysis C.M. Achilles, John Reynolds, and Susan Hoover

Judgment James Sweeney and Diana Bourisaw

Organizational Oversight Erlandson, Stark, and Ward

Implementation Anita M. Pankake

Delegation Michael Ward and Bettye MacPhail

The Programmatic Domains

Instruction and the Learning Environment James Keefe and John Jenkins

Staff Development Sally J. Zepeda

Student Guidance and Development Ward and Worsham

Measurement and Evaluation James F. McNamara and David A. Erlandson

Resource Allocation M. Scott Norton and Larry Kelly

The Interpersonal Domains

Motivating Others David P. Thompson

Interpersonal Sensitivity John R. Hoyle and Harrison M. Crenshaw

Oral and Nonverbal Expression Ivan Muse

Written Expression India J. Podsen, Charles Allen, Glenn Pethel, and John Waide

The Contextual Domains

Working in a Legal and Regulatory Environment: A Handbook for School Leaders David Sperry

Philosophical and Cultural Values George Crawford and Janice Nicklaus

ABOUT THE AUTHORS

George Crawford is an associate professor of Teaching and Leadership at the University of Kansas, Lawrence, where he teaches organizational theory, governance, and leadership to practicing and aspiring teachers, principals, and superintendents. He received the Bachelor of Fine Arts and Master of Education degrees from Ohio University and the Doctor of Philosophy degree from The Ohio State University. Prior to coming to Kansas, he taught vocal music and sixth grade in the public schools of West Virginia and Ohio. He has also served as an elementary principal, assistant high school principal, high school principal and school board member. He currently serves as the K.U. Professional Development School Liaison to J.C. Harmon High School in Kansas City, Kansas.

Janice Nicklaus is a staff development specialist in the Lawrence, Kansas, pubic schools. She received her Bachelor of Arts and Masters degrees from The Ohio State University and the Doctor of Philosophy from the University of Kansas. She has served as a public school teacher, coordinator for Title I math, and adjunct professor. Her work with school administrators includes conducting study groups, providing professional development on developmental supervision and related pedagogical issues and assisting building administrators with problem solving processes. She has written and edited monographs related to professional development and made presentations to professional audiences nationally.

TABLE OF CONTENTS

PREFACE

The *School Leadership Library* is dedicated to building principals' performance skills in ways that positively impact the learning of the students in their schools. There are probably few principals, teachers, or other school professionals who would not accept this as a worthy goal. But these same professionals would have much greater difficulty reaching a consensus about two questions that must be answered to fulfill this goal: (1) What is meant by a "positive impact" on student learning? (2) How should this impact be achieved? The other volumes in the *School Leadership Library* provide principals with much valuable information and direction for answering these questions; but they must also be answered individually by each principal. These answers must be guided by philosophical and cultural beliefs that begin with a clear understanding by the principal of his or her own values.

The principal's value system should guide every decision that is made in the school. As George Crawford and Janice Nicklaus point out in the first chapter of this volume, "all values are *not* equal." The principal's value system must be supportive of democratic principles and must be displayed, not only in their own actions and words but also in the regularities that are displayed by teachers, students, parents, and other school stakeholders.

In Chapter 2, the authors show the reader the value of "paradoxical thinking" in solving problems and provide directions on how paradoxical logic may be incorporated into the decision making of the school. They encourage principals to reflect on two, fundamentally different ways of viewing problems and to use this knowledge to develop appropriate leadership approaches to the various problems they encounter.

The third chapter provides the principal with some practical advice for ascertaining the consistency among values, beliefs, actions and democratic principles in the school's operation. In a democratic society, the school which prepares youth to take productive places in other institutions must itself be a "living laboratory for democracy."

Schools, the communities in which they exist, and the governance structures under which they operate are not uniformly supportive of democratic values or patterns of operation. The principal often finds these antidemocratic tendencies in direct conflict with the democratic principles that he or she is trying to foster in the school. Chapter 4 presents the principal with some tools for analyzing these conflicts and for determining what action can be taken to resolve issues in ways that best serve the democratic principles which the school espouses.

The final chapter of this volume demonstrates to principals the need for examining their own behavior for inconsistencies and incongruities. It also provides them with practical strategies and for creating approaches that maximize the "goodness of fit" between and among thoughts, words and actions. Principals are encouraged to find their voice so that they effectively articulate ideals to the school's various audiences. The book concludes with some practical advice for obtaining clarity among the various values espoused for the school and with an exhortation to continue examining values as a vehicle for building a consistent, pervasive argument for the incorporation of democratic principles into the school.

As we noted previously, the tools provided in this volume give valuable direction for applying the knowledge and skills presented in the other books of the *School Leadership Library.*

David A. Erlandson
Alfred P. Wilson

1

FROM BEDROCK TO SHIFTING SANDS

Once upon some future time, a certain person will set a hopeful foot on a promising path to the principalship. If you are that person, your success will be influenced in fundamental ways by philosophical and cultural beliefs. If those beliefs are to reflect a commitment to democracy, they must be firmly grounded in democratic principle.

The qualifying *if* is significant: *If* we are to be committed to democracy.... We hope everyone reading these words will find the qualifier unnecessary—almost an insult. "Of *course* we're committed to democracy. Who would ever have thought otherwise?"

Unfortunately, every despot throughout recorded history has thought otherwise. Because our purpose is to encourage the development of principled beliefs, it is essential to understand that the *central principle* upon which we rely is democratic, as embodied in rule *of, by,* and *for the people*—a rule that is unavoidably inefficient and messy at times, but one that also recognizes the necessity for tension between freedom and control and the importance of *voluntary, uncoerced* participation in civic affairs.

Principled behavior is grounded in and dependent on well-formed philosophical and cultural beliefs. Gutmann (1987) asserts that "principled educational policy" cannot be made "without exposing our principles and investigating their implications" (p. 6). The same assertion can be extended beyond policy to what we will call "principled principaling." In other words, principals who reflectively expose, investigate, and then settle their minds on relevant, *principled* beliefs increase their ca-

1

pacities for practicing in ways that are convincingly consistent with democracy.

Achieving this ideal requires careful reflection on the principles—those philosophical and cultural beliefs—that guide your actions. In terms that are more concrete: you need to be clear about the beliefs by which you live. While it seems overly dramatic, it is helpful to emphasize the point by addressing it from the perspective of an *extreme* possibility. In doing so, we posit that it seems reasonable to argue that *you should be clear about those beliefs for which you would die.* This proposition may alarm, but should be emphasized: Some future day may either offer the opportunity to *decide* whether to die, or may *demand* that you do so in service to some particular belief. It should be apparent that assertions about principals dying in defense of beliefs are more figurative and metaphorical than literal for the most part. While martyrdom is a remote possibility, thinking about the concept of self-sacrifice emphasizes the deep, weighty importance of values and beliefs in principals' lives and practice.

Acts that inspire awe because of their selfless, heroic qualities are products of a more or less conscious commitment to certain beliefs. The principal who *literally* dies in the crossfire of rival gangs while touring his school's neighborhood is as much a witting sacrifice to his commitments as innocent victim of anonymous violence. Senseless murder can be attributed to fate, but acts of this kind also are perversely and ironically predictable. They are caused in part by unwavering commitment to certain beliefs.

This assertion may seem unreasonably dogmatic. A logician might even argue that the *first* cause of the principal's death was a bullet, not beliefs. We suggest, however, that it was *belief* which caused him to be in harm's way in the first place. Bullets pose no threat to the principal whose beliefs do not nudge him, however subtly, to be in their paths.

AXIOMATIC TRUTHS

Axiomatic truths are essential ingredients in the achievement of acceptable agreements on value-laden issues. They are essential features of *all* efforts to understand situations where evidence is simply assumed to exist and not necessarily demonstrated or proved. Axioms, you may remember, are statements that are taken to be true without question or verification. An illustrative example is seen in "We hold these truths to be *self-evident*...."

SOURCES OF AXIOMATIC TRUTH

Axioms come down to us almost literally as passengers on conversations and other interactions between generations and as a consequence of consistencies between what we have been taught and what we observe. If we take an ancient and sentimental example such as *True love betrayeth not,* we can easily check the validity of the assertion against our experience. Have we witnessed examples of *true love*? If we have, we've observed that betrayal was not a feature of the relationship. We can usually satisfy ourselves that such things as loyalty, concern, kindness, consideration, support, and affection characterize loving relationships. The axiom, then, carried from great grandparent to grandparent, thence to parent, and finally to us, tends to be reinforced by both what we have heard and what we have seen. There may have been exceptions in our individual experience, but even then, we probably have witnessed enough in others' relationships to find the axiom plausible. In a somewhat simpler and more directly applicable sense, it is axiomatic that principals' students and staffs expect them to be trustworthy.

The *sources* of axiomatic truths tend to be *cultural*—sources that are deeply ingrained in the ethos, mores, and values of our particular social and cultural tradition. Some of the axiomatic elements of our collective cultural tradition are not subject to debate. Assertions about safety are illustrative. It is not a matter for cultural debate whether children should be safe, or whether schools should be safe places. The assertion is axiomatically true—accepted without proof.

Equality of opportunity also seems to be a fairly well-established element in our national conscience—at least nominally. Others are more controversial. The options represented by the ability to choose either (a) a prolife, (b) a prochoice, or (c) a position that is *both* prolife *and* prochoice give stark evidence of the potential for division where deeply held values are at work.

Should women have autonomous control over their bodies, including decisions about abortion, or should legislated positions prevail over individual choice?

Many of us prefer to avoid this kind of question. It must ultimately be resolved—if at all—based on values. Do the rights of the individual or those of the state prevail? Many of you will be called upon to give binding opinions on this question.

MECHANISMS AND PATTERNS OF CHANGE

As time passes, values change. That is—or seems to be—another axiom. Things that our forebears loved, we disdain. What was once celebrated becomes an object of indifference or scorn.

On one hand, children are almost sacred. On the other, they are discardable objects—"things" to be thrown away in the face of some narcissistic urge to exercise autonomous control.

It should be apparent that the issue is not that simple. Questions extending far beyond the possible role of narcissism are involved. Gross physical deformity, for example, makes some children's prospects of viable futures unequivocally remote. For some, in circumstances such as these, it seems at least insensitive to criticize *principled* support for prochoice behavior. Having said this, however, we also must recognize that it is customary in some parts of our culture to treat *all* life as sacred. These are the kinds of issues that forge unsettled, fragmented futures. They also are issues that contain or imply the kinds of questions that will inform, influence, and shape *your* core beliefs and values.

From one perspective, history appears to run seamlessly from era to era. From a slightly different perspective, history does not proceed seamlessly at all. Rather, it runs jarringly and disruptively from age to age, often as a consequence of ideological and material dominance—the breaching of the Berlin Wall by Western industrial strength, for instance—or technological breakthroughs of major significance. The invention of printing, the Industrial Revolution, the invention of the automobile, flight, and the emergence of the Information Age are all examples of the latter sort.

Change can be characterized in a number of ways. Whether we view it as the only constant; inevitable, innovative progress;

stimulating, disruptive, or paralyzingly frustrating, it *is* an irre-futable attribute or feature of existence. It also appears to be unarguably true that change is critically related to values. A person or group senses a better way of doing some particular thing. The "better way" may be related to any number of things: How we are encouraged to *think*, for example, in less dogmatic and more open-minded ways, how we might more effectively and efficiently provide some good—technology comes to mind—or service. Health care, education, and telecommunications are ready examples in this category. One of the more helpful things to remember about this process is the role of values *in* it, and their relationship *to it*. So far as *role* is concerned, it should be noted that values are a *necessary agent* in change. If there is no change in values, there is no motivating tension between what *is* and what *might* or *should* be. Without that tension, there will be no change. The *role* of values in change, then, might be thought of as catalytic.

Turning our attention to the *relationship* of values to change, it seems fitting to think of them as *necessary*—directly related *to* and required elements *in* change. In summary, then, we can say that values—ones that are *themselves* changed—are necessary precursors to and ingredients in change, and their role is analogous to that played by a catalyst. In other words, values are primary *mechanisms* in change processes. How might we think in useful ways about *patterns* in our consideration of *mechanisms and patterns of change*?

If we think of *pattern* as a model or guide—a way of looking at, thinking about, and understanding how some particular thing or phenomenon "works"—we can envision a rudimentary design which helps to clarify the patterned relationships of values and change. Let us begin thinking about the patterned relationships between values and change with a proposition that is intended to provide a simplified summary of what we are thinking about. Our proposal is this: *What we are thinking about may be summarized as processes and products.* In other words, change is made or brought about in, imposed on, or influenced in *processes*—thinking, for instance—and *products*—any *thing* that results from some *process*. Let's proceed from the proposition, then, to a consideration of *pattern*.

If we think of *patterns* in a conventional way, it probably will be helpful to remember that they provide directions for processes that have a beginning, an end, and essential intermediate steps or procedures. In making a garment or model airplane, we "begin" by buying or making a pattern or plan and purchasing needed materials. If we are as thoughtful as we should be, we'll satisfy ourselves before getting underway that we have all the requirements at hand: cloth, balsa, thread, cutting (or layout) board, scissors, razor blades, pins, thread, glue, and so forth. It also is helpful to remember that in all instances of change, some motivating force is required to set things in motion. In the case of the garment or model plane, it may simply be that we enjoy sewing or modeling, coupled with a more or less vague notion that we would like to have, or "need" some garment, flying model, or whatever. We then proceed in a stepwise—first, second, third, and so on—fashion to the realization of our aim.

As we think of how these patterns are achieved in schools, it is beneficial to recognize that *change*—call it *school reform, school improvement,* or *curricular reform*—brings about some alteration or modification in the *status quo* or present condition. In simplified form, the *pattern* begins to take shape when some *value-driven motivation* arises which creates an awareness, or raises the possibility that the *status quo* might be advantageously modified. It is also helpful to remember that the value-driven motivation can be viewed from a systems perspective as arising *either* within *or* outside of, or *both* within *and* outside of the school. A teacher or other staff member, parent, or some other "system insider" might be the source of motivation for change. Some person or agency "outside" the school also can be the motivating force—the school district, state department of education, diocese, or federal source, for example. In its simplest form, the pattern of change can be viewed as analogous to that displayed in Figure 1.1.

FIGURE 1.1 A SIMPLIFIED PATTERN OF SCHOOL CHANGE

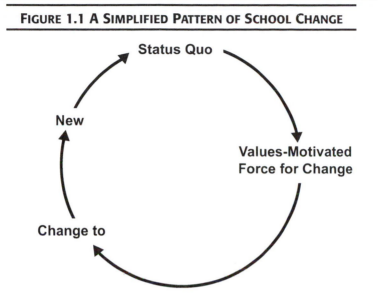

As you can see from Figure 1.1, change begins with an established set of circumstances called the *status quo*, or "state at which." In a school, this state obviously might range from stable to chaotic, positive to negative, acceptable to unacceptable, or any number of other contrasting, descriptive word-pairs. You might want to pause here, in fact, and identify others that could describe the *status quo* or present state. Having done so, you will see that as you move around the circle clockwise from *status quo*, you first encounter a *Values-Motivated Force for Change*. In the case of our school, we may find that some member of the school's immediate community—a system insider—has noted that the status quo is really good overall, but that some particular aspect could be made even better. This is the point where *values* and *values-motivated forces* come into play. The "insider," working from a value which says "Good things can usually be improved," may have recognized that changing how students enter the lunchroom will reduce congestion in the school's corridors while also reducing serving time *and* improving the atmosphere in the cafeteria. A plan is devised, students and staff are briefed on the *change*, and the *change* to a *new status quo* is implemented.

As you think about how status quo, motivating forces, changes, and transitions to new status quos are accomplished, it is helpful to recognize that this oversimplified description disguises and conceals the complex nature of real-school environments. The lunchroom is only one of many parts of the complex system we recognize as a school. There may be a transportation system (or subsystem), curriculum subsystem, grade-level or other *organizational* subsystem, discipline subsystem, physical plant subsystem, and so forth. All of these subsystems interact and affect each other. Change in one will very likely bring about one or more changes in one or more of the related subsystems, and these may be anticipated or surprising, helpful or harmful. What is important to note is this: As you think about change and the role played in it by values, remember that a simplified model must be expanded if it is to be useful in real settings. If the pattern or model of how change and values interact is to be practical, you need to be mindful that adequate representation requires not just one, but many models. Our primary point, though, is to encourage thinking about how the basic mechanism works.

Let us refocus, then, on how time runs more or less smoothly or jarringly, from era to era, and from status quo to new status quo. Our present era bears witness to an apparent change in people's tendencies to identify patriotically with our nation. What might formerly have been called a general tendency for people to proudly identify with country and patriotic symbol now appears to have been supplanted by more narrowly focused special interests and the shrill, nonnegotiable demands often associated with special interest groups. General welfare seems to have taken a back seat to self-interest.

Profound, deep change in core values is painful, disruptive, and divisive. The deliberate taking of life in our culture, for example, is hotly debated. Yet, we prosecute persons who violate laws against assisting suicide and at the same time defend laws that permit abortion. These two practices appear to reflect values that are in direct conflict. To help a person die who *wishes* to die is proscribed; *causing* a person to die who has no say in the matter, as in abortion, is *legal*. Where will a consideration of democratic principle lead us on this issue?

It seems reasonable to entertain the possibility that laws which are inconsistent to the point of mutual contradiction may be culturally damaging, inasmuch as the apparent contradictions breed cynicism and loss of respect for law. Some choose to think that the right of women to autonomous control over their bodies is to be preferred to the butchery that occurred prior to *Roe v. Wade*, while wishing profoundly that respect for life, actual or potential, had not declined so precipitously. That, however, cannot conceal the obvious: People disagree bitterly and violently over what comprises the greater good in the matter—the mother's right or the unborn's right? The right of the would-be suicide or the right of the state? Whatever we may believe in these matters, it is impossible to ignore the contradiction entailed in practices that make it both permissible and prohibited for doctors (or others) to kill. A culture that cannot reconcile differences of this sort threatens to consume itself. In fact, it may fail to qualify as a culture at all, inasmuch as it does not *share* common values.

THE ROLE OF EXAMPLE SETTING

Example setting is a tacit feature of this narrative, which needs to be made explicit and imperative. It is a relatively simple thing to articulate, but perhaps not so simple in its implementation.

In plain terms, the imperative suggests that all of us should be mindful of the fact that we set examples. It also seems important to point out that this assertion contains yet another axiom. That axiom suggests that we are *always* modeling—whether we are conscious of it or not. Modeling, it can be axiomatically stated, is a more or less voluntary or *conscious* thing. It happens, whether we will it or not.

So it is with philosophical and cultural beliefs and values. We have them whether we intend to or not. Given that we have them, and given that others will notice (whether we intend them to or not), it follows that it will be beneficial if our beliefs are *principled*—that is, clearly related to meritorious principles in compelling ways.

"Well," you say. "Who gave *you* the right to rule the world? Who said it was okay for *you* to say what a meritorious principle was, and who appointed *you* to set the standards on making principles clear and compelling?" And you are right, of course. No one gave us, nor does anyone "give" anyone else the right to *dictate*—at least in a democracy. But also—*especially* in democracies—we establish covenants that govern our relationships (Sergiovanni, 1995) and, to a considerable extent, the very values that influence those covenants. In a democracy, each of us has the right to attempt to *persuade* the rest of us to think, feel, believe, and otherwise act in certain ways, and the rest of us have the right—within consensual limits—to voluntarily comply. The important point is that those who are most persistently articulate and visible also tend to be the most persuasive. Democracy *depends* on the *principled qualities* evident in the beliefs of persuasive people. "Democracy is justified," according to Strike, Haller, and Soltis (1988), "because it shows respect for persons" (p. 99). It follows that it is generally better for everyone if articulate, persuasive people are also highly principled. We take *principled* to mean *based on general truths or laws that are basic to other truths* (see "principle" in the *New International Webster's Comprehensive Dictionary*, 1996, p. 1003). It also should be evident that our intent here includes meanings that connote *appropriateness* and *beneficiality* of values and beliefs. While some might argue, for example, that Hitler and Stalin were "principled," we would reject them as exemplars because their values and beliefs—*principles,* if you will—were not appropriate and beneficial. On the contrary, their values and beliefs created legacies of hardship, terror, and destruction. For our purposes here, they would be exemplars of *un*principled values, belief, and behavior.

ADAPTATION WITHOUT DECAY AND COMPROMISE

None of us has to read many references to their waffling to become cynical about certain politicians. Similarly, none of us has to reflect too long on dealings with inconsistent coworkers and acquaintances to remember how frustrating and counterproductive it is to be told one thing today and the opposite thing tomorrow. The memorable negative consequences of inconsistency provide markers that help distinguish it from its recognizable opposite.

Consistency, on the other hand, is memorialized by references to its importance in people with whom "you always knew where you stood." It comes across in those who have effectively mastered it as integrity, dependability, predictability, solidity, comfort, and trustworthiness. It also is an important attribute of principled practice and is illustrated by such comments as, "Oh, so-and-so would never *dream* of doing that! It's a matter of *principle* with her!" The thing never to be dreamed of might involve a lie, a falsification of a record, or avoiding a confrontation necessary to maintain individual welfare or organizational health. In other words, something would be entailed that is dishonest, unethical, unprincipled, or otherwise not *right*—something which erodes the human condition. It will be expedient, rather than appropriate.

How does one "keep up with the times" in the adaptation of democratic principles to cultural change? As the comments on consistency suggest, a place to begin thinking about keeping up is found in this question: "Is it possible to identify a group of core values having the potential to bridge generations and cultures—that stand the test of time?"

Rushworth M. Kidder (1994) distilled a thoughtful collection of eight values that "...constitute a global code of values. Not *the* code, but *a* code" (p. 309). Those eight values are *love, truthfulness, fairness, freedom, unity, tolerance, responsibility,* and *respect for life*. As you reflect on these values, you will no doubt recognize that certain of them—unity and tolerance, for example—can seriously conflict with religious, ethnocentric, and nationalistic preferences. Similarly, love, truthfulness, fairness, and freedom may be viewed by hard-nosed competitors as naive and soft—attributes of weakness. It's a dog-eat-dog world, after all, and only the pious and writers of personal development books can afford to live according to such unrealistic values. Moreover, respect for life is equivocal, isn't it, or at least at odds with freedom of choice? We could probably all agree on responsibility—it's *necessary*. It makes the world go round!

You recognize, of course, that we're being a bit playful. If you are to be a *principled* principal—to found your practice on bedrock rather than shifting sand—your intention is aided by identifying selected core values that can prevail against the slippery tides of time. Kidder's list is a worthwhile compilation of candidates for such a collection. You can test this assertion by comparing each value with its opposite: love or hate; fairness or injustice; freedom or control; unity or division, and so forth. Remember the necessity of *ranking* values—*ordering* them—in order to decide. As a starting point, Kidder's list is consistent with democratic principle, inasmuch as the values he nominates for inclusion do not conflict with principles inherent in the terms, *by the people, of the people, and for the people.*

As we adapt our values in ways intended to avoid their decay and decline—becoming outdated—it is important to use defensible core values as both anchors and templates against which we evaluate changes we may be considering. Key questions include, Is the change consistent with democratic principle? Can I make this change without risking a serious compromise in a matter of conscience? Can I do what is proposed without damaging my integrity? Can the change be undertaken without intruding in undemocratic ways on the freedom of those who will be affected?

There will be times when a perceived obligation to act on a matter of principle will entail self-sacrifice: "Teachers and students are entitled to work in safety. Therefore, I will physically protect them if necessary." Knowing that offering protection may result in your own injury or death, you may conclude that other obligations—to family and future students, for example—argue against placing yourself at risk. That sort of thinking, however, should also encourage you to consider the possibility that your *failure* to protect may be labeled cowardice and lead to your dismissal.

THE CENTRALITY OF VALUE

We would argue that it is axiomatic—self-evidently true —that all values and beliefs are *not* equal. In fact, choosing (and decisions of every other kind) *depends* on the ability of the chooser to rank value preferences attached to different alternatives. Just as we might be convinced about the nature of reality—as Bishop Berkeley (ca 1710) was—by kicking a rock and having pain in our toe, we are convinced that certain things *must be true* if we are to develop a helpful understanding of phenomena, as confusing as the competing values may be.

Having posited that all values are *not* equal, we expect there surely will be someone who reads the assertion, gives a knowing look, and then gravely announces that everything—or *almost* everything—is relative. Conditions change. Under one set of circumstances a certain thing *might* work, but, if things *change*.... Most of us have heard these arguments and many of us believe similar things, not entirely without reason. Nevertheless, we emphasize that *the ability to choose* depends *on palpable differences in the values associated with different alternatives.* This is the first, critical leg of an essential axiom. The second leg is: *If different alternatives do not* have *palpably different values, then, any consideration of choosing between or among them is technically absurd*—in other words, a defiance of logic, and therefore an obvious waste of time.

PICKING OUR VALUES

Carlson (1996) suggests that the ability to discriminate among alternative values requires that we first make a critical distinction between *right* and *good:*

> Good refers to what is enjoyable, likable, or pleasurable, whereas right is proper, moral, and duty-bound. Good is already known by our preferences and does not have to be explained to us. It is basically hedonistic, part of our psychology of seeking pleasure and avoiding pain; it suffers from little inner conflict but can cause conflict externally in interpersonal relations (p. 160).

In attempting to become a *principled* principal, it seems entirely reasonable to expect that the success of the venture will be determined by one's ability to "act rightly." What does this mean?

Among other things, it means acting in accordance with principles of fairness, justice, honesty, trustworthiness, and liberty—principles that are certainly consistent with the overarching concept of democracy. To "act rightly" will sometimes entail acting in ways that are more difficult than easy, more self-threatening than self-protective, more concerned with general welfare than with special interests. It may require acting in ways that make you unpopular with friends or with powerful and potentially vindictive superiors. At times, it may require more courage than you think you have.

It will certainly require that you deal with all persons in an evenhanded way, to treat people who are identifiably different in ways that are consistent, appropriate, and fair. It strongly recommends meting out justice, opportunity, access, and other democratic rights in measures that are apportioned without regard for trait, tendency, or temperament.

Formal and Practical Arguments for Consistency

Three logical conventions will be of enormous help to the principled principal. The first is the use of syllogisms (e.g., Mammals are warm-blooded, have hair, and suckle their young. *Homo sapiens* are warm-blooded, have hair, and suckle their young. *Homo sapiens* are mammals.). The second is the central role played in logical analysis by making critical distinctions among *all, some,* and *none* (see Carroll, 1977). The third is the necessity in formal argument for premises and conclusions, and to have them related in compelling ways.

The role of syllogistic, or deductive, reasoning can be illustrated in this way. Let us suppose that you need to evaluate some prospective action or decision for its consistency with democratic principle—a decision, say, about whether middle-school cheerleaders (a) should be selected competitively and (b) whether, once chosen, they should be required to pay for their own uniforms.

The illustration is helpfully undertaken with a reminder from Strike, Haller, and Soltis (1988). They tell us "A decision is made democratically if:

1. The interests of each individual are fairly considered [and]

2. Each individual has a fair influence on the decision" (p. 94).

Note that both of the decision criteria contain the words *each* and *fair(ly)*. *Each* is the functional equivalent of *all* or *everyone*. In addressing the first, competition-related part of the question, it is necessary to ask whether *every student's interests* were fairly *considered*. This obviously is not synonymous with asking, "Does every student who *wishes* to cheer *get* to cheer?" It is, however, *emphatically* synonymous with taking pains to ensure that the selection process avoids features that systematically bias certain students' chances of being selected or rejected. This relates to the second criterion, and it obligates the principled principal to evaluate the selection process to be satisfied, for example, that organizers have not designed it in ways that elevate certain students' chances of selection while at the same time depressing others' chances. In other words, is the system *fair*? Are the interests of *all* students *fairly* considered? Were the students involved in decisions about the selection process in ways that enabled them to fairly influence the selection decisions? Do certain identifiable individuals or groups have so much power that consideration of individual interests and exercise of individual influence will be precluded?

Principled principals can rephrase the second part of the question in ways that illustrate the role of syllogism in applying democratic evaluative criteria. For example, you could ask whether *all* qualified cheerleader applicants should be permitted to cheer without regard for their ability to purchase a uniform. You also could ask: "In a democracy, is it appropriate for *some* otherwise qualified applicants to be excluded because of inability to pay?" You also could be alert to the existence in procedural descriptions of such language as: "*No* successful applicant will be denied the opportunity to cheer because he or she cannot afford a uniform."

As you think about the role of syllogistic reasoning in the *principled* application of your beliefs and values you might consider how temporal references could be helpfully integrated into formal argument. The temporal equivalents of *all, some,* and *none* are *always, sometimes,* and *never.* They can be combined in appropriate ways with premises and conclusions with the following kinds of illustrative results.

♦ Because democratic principles always reflect respect for individuals [*premise*], genuinely democratic schools will never adopt policies or practices that
  threaten to expose individuals to anything less than
  respectful treatment [*conclusion*].

♦ While it is true that the interests of individuals are
  always considered in democratic decision-making
  [*premise*], it is nevertheless possible that individuals
  will sometimes fail to achieve a preferred outcome
  [*conclusion*].

THE SELF-CONTRADICTORY NATURE OF MORAL RELATIVISM

Self-contradiction in an individual is sometimes disappoint-
ing, often confusing, and usually embarrassing. When a philosophical value or belief contradicts itself, the phenomenon
tends to lead predictably to related inconsistencies in behavior.
While it is evident that there are such things as paradoxes, and
while it also is true that there are productive, logical ways of
dealing with paradox (as we argue in Chapter 2), it nevertheless
tends to be necessary to recognize differences among competing
principles and goods. Our position, perhaps not surprisingly, is
that a morally relativistic attitude—one that views moral beliefs
as interchangeable according to circumstance—cannot comfort-
ably and helpfully coexist with the idea of principled principaling.

Having posited that moral relativism is not a tenable position for principled principals, and anticipating the concern of
some readers that we are being indefensibly dogmatic, let us try
to clarify the notion. We would say, first, that the proposition
"All moral goods and principles are not equal" does not dimin-
ish the importance of remembering to scrutinize all sweeping
generalizations! You remember examples of the warning words
you were advised to be on the lookout for: *all, every, always,
never.*

You also remember examples of the kinds of sweeping gen-
eralization you were advised to suspect: *Every* child deserves a
pony. *All* of us who have failed have derived benefits from the
experience. Successful schools *always* reflect the attributes re-

vealed by the effective schools research. Inappropriate behavior should *never* be ignored.

These are some mundane examples. A more important and influential example would be: "All values are equal." This, of course, is a relativistic position that is contradicted based on compelling evidence. All values are *not* equal, and the inference, which is logically drawn, is:

> Principals whose behavior is consistently and obviously principled have a clear understanding of attributes, which make some beliefs more essential than others. They understand that virtuous conduct adds more value to the human condition than morally depraved conduct, for example.

THE PRINCIPLED PRINCIPAL

ALIGNING THOUGHTS, WORDS, AND ACTIONS

Principled principals display leadership behavior that is clearly consistent with high moral purpose. That is to say, they act consistently on the basis of right, good, fair, just, and otherwise democratic purpose. We take these terms, respectively, to mean *conformable to moral law; satisfactory in quality; showing no partiality;* and *righteous, upright, honest* (see *New International Webster's Comprehensive Dictionary*, 1996, for more complete definitions). All of these terms are consistent with values that are associated with people of irreproachable reputation and ethical practice. In short, the principled principal is a person clothed with integrity.

Important components of principled practice are the quality and quantity of alignment or integration of what and how you *think,* the manner in which you *talk* about your thoughts, and the ways in which you *act* on your thoughts and words. The principled principal behaves in ways that display a seamless integration of thought, talk, and action. This principal is the opposite of the one whose actions speak so loudly you cannot hear what they say.

PROFESSIONALS, ETHICS, AND PROFESSIONAL ETHICS

A late philosopher colleague was fond of saying that professional is one of the few words in English requiring no modifiers. If you reflect on it for a moment, you may come to agree with the assertion.

> In summary, *a professional orientation* is characterized by technical competence acquired through long training; adherence to a set of professional norms that includes a service ideal, objectivity, impersonality, and impartiality; a colleague-oriented reference group; autonomy in professional decision making; and self-imposed control based upon knowledge, standards, and peer review. (Hoy & Miskel, 1987, p. 150)

A professional, according to Hoy and Miskel's summary, displays great skill—technical competency—in a particular field. Principals and other educators are not generally recognized in the literature as *professionals.* This, according to Hoy and Miskel (1987), is because "[s]emiprofessional organizations are primarily concerned with the communication of knowledge, rather than its creation; their professionals generally do not have the guarantee of privileged communication. Elementary schools constitute the most common example of the semiprofessional organization" (p. 152). While grounds presently may be lacking to claim full professional status for principals and other educators, we would still encourage readers to adopt, as a value, the goal of full professional status.

If we contemplate the case of the principal, we may agree that the *professional* practitioner is indeed one who has acquired virtuosic mastery over a vast, complex array of knowledge and skill. This person commands expertise in curriculum and instruction, instructional leadership, education law, human motivation, interpersonal relations, conflict resolution, educational measurement and evaluation, planning, financial management, organizational behavior, problem solving/decision making, total quality management, human development, youth gangs,

and a host of related topics. *Professional* command of these topics, fields, areas, or concerns, moreover, reveals itself as the flu-
ent, fluid, confident, and reasonably effortless ability to address
routine and exceptional situations in effective, satisfying ways.
All of this, of course, is buttressed by and grounded on an assumption that all of these impressive feats will be carried out in
ways that are clearly and unequivocally ethical. In fact, our late
colleague would have said that it is not only *unnecessary* to say
ethical professional, but redundant. That, however, is not the
same as saying that it is redundant to consider the role of ethics
within the context of professionalism.

Ethics, according to the *American Heritage Dictionary, 2nd ed.*
(1985), is variously defined as "The study of the general nature
of morals and of the specific moral choices to be made by the individual in his relationship with others, [and t]he rules or standards governing the conduct of the members of a profession" (p.
467). If we look to professional associations for examples, we
find that the *Statement of Ethics for School Administrators* of the
National Association of Elementary School Principals (1976) begins with a preamble:

> An educational administrator's professional behav-
> ior must conform to an ethical code. The code must
> be idealistic and at the same time practical, so that it
> can apply reasonably to all educational administra-
> tors. The administrator acknowledges that the
> schools belong to the public they serve for the pur-
> pose of providing educational opportunities to all.
> However, the administrator assumes responsibility
> for providing professional leadership in the school
> and community. This responsibility requires the ad-
> ministrator to maintain standards of exemplary pro-
> fessional conduct. It must be recognized that the ad-
> ministrator's actions will be viewed and appraised
> by the community, professional associates, and stu-
> dents. To these ends, the administrator subscribes to
> the following statements of standards.

Ten ethical standards are listed after the phrase "The educational administrator:" Just the first two are included here for illustrative purposes.

1. Makes the well-being of students the fundamental value in all decision making and actions.

2. Fulfills professional responsibilities with honesty and integrity.

A review of the complete list of ethical standards demonstrates their clear advocacy for the exercise of judgment that consistently indicates understanding of the differences between right and wrong. The standards also make it abundantly clear that this ethical code obligates the principal to not just *understand* the difference between right and wrong, but also to act in ways that reflect a respectable character.

CRITERIAL ATTRIBUTES OF MORAL LEADERSHIP

The approach to teaching referred to as "attaining concepts" will be recognized by those who have studied Joyce and Weil's *Models of Teaching* (1986). Joyce and Weil use an anecdote to illustrate the notion of "attribute." The anecdote involves a college senior describing her "ideal man" to a friend. The friend eventually concludes that the senior likes "short men who laugh a lot, and…tend[s] to avoid men who are very good students" (p. 27). Joyce and Weil then cite Bruner, Goodnow, and Austin's (1967) definition of the process of concept attainment: "the search for and listing of attributes that can be used to distinguish exemplars from nonexemplars of various categories" (p. 233).

The idea or concept of attribute, or *criterial* attribute, is a tool that is required to understand new, unfamiliar ideas and concepts. Moral leadership might be an example of a new, unfamiliar concept. If so, it is appropriate to ask what attributes set *moral* leadership apart from leadership that is immoral or amoral. In other words, how can we distinguish exemplars of moral leadership from nonexemplars? What are the criterial attributes that allow us to make the distinction?

You may be inclined to say that the answer to the question is self-evident; *everyone* knows what it means to be a moral person and to provide moral leadership. A devoted postmodernist might even hold the question to be meaningless, given that morality is (a) situational, (b) relative, and (c) in the eye of the beholder—something for which each of us constructs our own distinctive meaning or meanings according to environment, time, and mood.

We continue to hold that moral leadership is an essential component of good, successful, effective schools. It is both something that "you know when you see" and "see when you know." As a rule, moral leadership is not something that varies from situation to situation. It tends, rather, to be a constant in the kinds of schools most of us would like all students to attend. Its attributes, not surprisingly, tend to coincide to a considerable extent with the attributes of democratic and ethical behavior.

A helpful consideration of attributes that allow us to distinguish between *moral* leadership and leadership that is *not* moral really must begin with the meaning of *moral*. The first definition in *New International Webster's Comprehensive Dictionary* (1996) is *pertaining to character and behavior from the point of view of right and wrong* (p. 826). It is important to recognize that our ability to distinguish what is moral, according to the definition, depends on a general notion of what distinguishes right from wrong. In other words, if we are unable or unwilling to make value judgments about things that are right or appropriate, and things that are wrong or inappropriate, we either deliberately or by default forfeit the ability to make qualitative judgments. If that ability is forfeited, we cannot say such things as "That's good for you" or "That's bad for you" with the expectation that they will be instrumentally meaningful or helpful to anyone. We are aware that some instances of right and wrong tend to lie along a continuum where, at one extreme, an action is more clearly right or wrong than it will tend to be toward the middle of the continuum. If we take stealing as an example, we will *usually* judge stealing to be wrong, but in the case of a parent who has become impoverished by external circumstance it is not so *clearly* wrong when that person steals to feed her starving child. Instances of this sort make it clear that certain values are sometimes tempered by or *relative to* circumstance. Let that be stipulated, though, while we move on to consideration of attributes of *moral leadership*.

The moral leader is *just*—upright, impartial, and legitimate; *honest*—fair and candid in dealing with others; and *respectful*—deferential. The moral leader is *loving*—affectionate and devoted; *kind*—gentle, tender, good-hearted, and humane; and *trustworthy*—worthy of confidence, reliable. The moral leader is *responsible*—answerable legally or morally for the discharge of a duty, trust, or debt. As we think of the attributes of the moral leader, we also must consider that the moral leader is *tolerant*—long-suffering, indulgent, liberal. The moral leader is *vigilant*—alert, watchful, heedful. The moral leader is *courageous*—brave, daring. The moral leader is *consistent*—congruous and compatible, not self-contradictory. The moral leader is sensitive and considerate. Are any definitions really required for these terms? The moral leader has *integrity*—is of unimpaired state. The moral leader has *earned* respect. The emphasis here, of course, is on *earned*. *Respect* means to have deferential regard for, or to trust: to defer to the superior judgment of one who is apparently wiser. The moral leader also is thought of as having *presence* or *bearing*—"something invisible, but near and sensible." The moral leader has *character*—high qualities, moral force, reputation—and is *virtuous*—morally pure and good. In fact, we would probably say that moral leadership is an attribute of character, and character, as we know, is an attribute about which prospective employers seek references. (Consult *Webster's Comprehensive Dictionary*, 1996, for references to definitions used above.)

Let us suppose that we wanted to inspect a sample of principaling to see whether it survived scrutiny for evidence of moral leadership; that is, to see whether the principaling was *principled!* The sample that we have in mind involved a school program intended to encourage children to read. Children who read at least two books were to receive recognition and rewards, and a thoughtful teacher devised a means by which even non-readers could be acknowledged—by having books read *to* them. The project concluded and every child had either read two books or had two books read to them. As it turned out, the children who had been read to were not recognized at the assembly held to cap the program. Moreover, the teachers who decided to withhold recognition from nonreaders also withheld treats from the nonreaders at a class party following the recognition assembly.

The teacher who had arranged for all children to achieve success in reading was understandably disappointed and angered at the colleagues' unilateral and arbitrary decision to withhold recognition and an expected treat from the nonreaders. Assuming that the disappointed teacher expressed concern to the principal, which of the following responses from the principal align best with attributes of moral leadership?

1. "I'll talk with them, but I doubt they'll do anything."

2. "Well, they've both taught here for a long time, and I don't think I can change them."

3. "What happened to the nonreaders was terrible. The damage is done, unfortunately, but I'll conference with the other teachers and put a written reprimand in their files."

4. "I'm glad you brought this to my attention. The children are entitled to fair treatment—especially since they'd expected being read to to count. I'll talk with the teachers immediately about the inappropriateness of their actions. I'll also direct them to apologize to the kids and provide an immediate treat."

ON BECOMING A MORAL LEADER

The essence of one of the principal components of the process of becoming a moral leader is captured by a tale of a chicken and a pig. It seems that the chicken invited the pig to accompany her to the farmhouse so that they might participate in breakfast. Pig declined, and was immediately accused of being fainthearted. "Easy for you to say," pig observed. "*Your* participation merely requires you to be *involved*. *My* participation, on the other hand, requires full *commitment!*"

So it is with becoming a moral leader: full commitment is required. One can read helpful materials ranging from classical and medieval texts to contemporary scholarship. The classical literature includes Aristotle's *Nichomachean Ethics,* a primer in the study of morality. St. Thomas Aquinas's multivolume *Summa Theologiae* (orig. 1485) includes materials that are of instrumental use in formulating a code of moral behavior. In the introduction to the volume on courage, for example, St. Thomas confronts us with the notion that courage, prudence, justice, and temperance are "the four cardinal virtues." "Virtues are dispositions which facilitate the direction of human energies, in harmony with right reason, towards their full development in an integrated personality" (p. xxii). Kohlberg (1983) provides means for assessing our "level" of moral reasoning, and Beck and Murphy (1994) reopen the study of ethics as a contemporary concern in the preparation of educational leaders.

All of these sources are useful, but the story of the chicken and the pig gives needed emphasis to the role of commitment in moral practice. Committed moral practice is a serious, daunting, and demanding prospect. St. Thomas, for example, points out that the supreme expression of courage—one of the "cardinal virtues"—is martyrdom. He also cites Cicero's assertion that "courage is undertaking dangers and enduring toils after full reflection" (p. 11); that is, to go consciously and deliberately into harm's way, knowing that the choice may result in personal unpleasantness, hardship, or death. This reminder of the possibly fatal consequences of committing oneself to a highly moral kind of leadership gives bold emphasis to the need for accurate knowledge of self as the commitment is contemplated. Self-examination, self-scrutiny, and self-reflection certainly are imperative activities for anyone who is weighing the consequences and costs of committed moral leadership.

All of this suggests that the process undertaken by an individual becoming a moral leader is both a matter of conscience and a matter of empirical evidence. The critical role of *conscience* is illustrated by recalling folk-like phrases that rely on the term for their impact: "I cannot in good *conscience* do that." "As my *conscience* is my guide, I must do the right thing here." Its role is implied by such phrases as: "I couldn't *live* with myself if...."

Recalling and sharing memorable instances of the exercise of conscience fills in the empirical evidence side of the ledger most effectively. Some will recall the lasting impression created by the heroic teacher who confronted a tyrannical, violent parent in order to bring badly needed calm to a terrified child. Others may remember a kind, determined person who would not allow a comparatively weak person to be exploited by one who was both stronger and unprincipled. Using these two general examples as guides, see whether you can identify additional examples from your own experience. You may find it challenging. Displays of conscience are rare enough to be remarkable and their rarity may make their recollection difficult. If the task seems impossible, try substituting such words as *will, determination, character,* and *integrity* for *conscience.*

EXERCISE: WHAT ARE MY DYING PLACES?

We intend to use the term *dying place* in a metaphorical way. But, in announcing that intent, we hasten to remind you and ourselves that the metaphor sometimes becomes real. Recall the example of the principal who was killed by gang crossfire. Too many alarming accounts exist of principals and other school personnel being brutally assaulted or murdered to deny that violence and a violent end are possibilities for the principal—remote, perhaps, but possible. Consequently, it may be essential to make the first entry in the dying place exercise an acknowledgment of the possibility of dying, literally, by virtue of our presence in the principalship. The remaining items are intended to encourage and promote conscious reflection on and discussion of the notion that there are a variety of value-laden, morally charged problems and issues that challenge principals in conscience-burdening ways. Think about the examples listed below and then decide whether you would be "not at all" or "very likely" inclined to act in a morally principled way in dealing with the issue; that is, to "to go the mat" or "die" (metaphorically, we hope) over it.

How Likely Would I Be to Die Over

1. Adults abusing children and youth entrusted to my care?

    Not at all   •   •   •   •   •   •   *Very likely*

2. Federal, state, or local mandates thought to be inappropriate for students?

    Not at all • • • • • • *Very likely*

3. Parent or patron threat to a member of my staff?

    Not at all • • • • • • *Very likely*

4. Being given a threatening ultimatum over a student's failure to win a desired role?

    Not at all • • • • • • *Very likely*

5. Being offered a bribe to allow an ineligible student to enroll in my school?

    Not at all • • • • • • *Very likely*

6. Being ordered to follow an unethical directive by a superior?

    Not at all • • • • • • *Very likely*

7. Being ordered by a gang to ignore their presence in my school?

    Not at all • • • • • • *Very likely*

8. Protecting a communication where I had promised confidentiality?

    Not at all • • • • • • *Very likely*

9. Overhearing a colleague make a racist remark about a student or colleague?

    Not at all • • • • • • *Very likely*

10. A compelling parent-accusation of unethical behavior by one of my staff?

    Not at all • • • • • • *Very likely*

As you think about your responses to the items, you may want to add others of your own. You may feel strongly committed to equality of educational opportunity. Would you be willing to compromise that value? You may feel morally and legally committed to ensure that children with handicaps have fully inclusive access to appropriate educational experiences. To what lengths will you go to provide inclusive experiences? You may be conscientiously committed to be vigilant about the quality of instruction in your school and to take extreme measures if necessary to maintain it. Would you compromise that value if it became apparent that the favorite relative of your most vindictive board of education member had proven to be irremediably incompetent?

SUMMARY

In this introductory chapter, we raised issues that will sensitize aspiring and practicing principals and assistant principals to what might be called the profoundly grave, or gravely profound, importance of philosophical and cultural values and beliefs. We referred to contemporary practices—abortion and euthanasia—which are violently divisive. In doing so, we intended to cite examples that rely on values-based beliefs that lead, in their extreme manifestations, to rancorous conflict.

In the real world of principals' practice, these admittedly contentious issues may never rise to the level of everyday concern. They do represent, however, exemplars of the *kinds* of issues that challenge practitioners in career-threatening ways. We therefore encourage you to think deeply about them.

We also introduced a notion that is central to the theme of this book—that differences in values are real, essential elements of your ability to identify "bedrock" values that will ground your practice. This proposition, of course, relies for its plausibility on the additional notion that *not all values and beliefs are interchangeably equivalent.* In other words, if all values are equivalent, it is impossible to determine the alternative results of choice upon which choice depends. Values and beliefs, make no mistake about it, *do* make a difference!

Our intent in this chapter—and in the remainder of the book—is to emphasize the *real, profound differences* that values and beliefs make in human existence. In saying this, we especially want to emphasize the significant differences that exist between the realities of demanding practice and the latitudes of scholarly discourse. The lives of principals' everyday practice can be eerily challenging. These realities exist in sharp contrast to the "neutral objectivity" of scholars' assessments of what practitioners face. Your lives, in reality, can be bloody enterprises. In the immediate moments of "needs to decide," you will not have recourse to much more than your accumulated knowledge, your skill, and your "wits." What we provide here is some grounding to make your knowledge comforting, your skill adequate, and your wits sharp.

ACTION FOLLOW-UP

◆ List five or six values and beliefs that provide central, primary direction for your life. After you've listed them, carefully review them and write two or three sentences that describe how these particular values or beliefs became influential for you. Talk specifically about whether your primary values and beliefs tend to be axiomatic—accepted without proof—or are grounded in evidence that you can use as arguments to support your choices.

◆ Think of one colleague whose values and beliefs have powerfully and positively influenced your development as an educator. Describe those values and beliefs, and explain why and how they influenced your professional behavior.

◆ If you are in a class or workshop, tentatively identify two or three persons with whom you believe you could work effectively in a school because your values and beliefs are complementary. Specify what you heard or saw that influenced your choices. File away your choices for future use.

◆ Complete the "How Likely Would I Be to Die Over" exercise. Compare and discuss your choices with one other person who has completed the exercise. Emphasize similarities and differences in your respective values and beliefs that appear to account for or explain those similarities and differences.

2

PARADOX

"Administration" combines two Latin terms: *ad,* meaning "to" or "toward," and *minister,* meaning "to attend to the wants and needs of others" (*The American Heritage Dictionary, 2nd ed.* 1985, p. 80). Administration, then, means "acting toward others in ways that address their needs and wants." This appears to be relatively simple and straightforward. From one perspective we can say that if we understand what it means to "administer," we should know whether we are *either* doing it *or* not. We can also take the view that we are administering in ways that are *more* or *less* in keeping with the meaning of the term. In other words, we might say that we are *both* administering as we *should, and* administering as we should *not*!

Administrative behavior that is consistent with what Sergiovanni (1992) calls "servant leadership" appears to be consistent with the literal meaning of "administration." "Servant leadership is more easily provided if the leader understands that serving others is important but that the most important thing is to serve the values and ideas that help shape the school as a covenantal community" (p. 125). Covenants, as we know, are compact-like agreements. The administration of binding organizational agreements requires leadership that reflects sensitive, appropriate attention to democratic principle. Democratic leadership connotes beliefs and practices that also are congruent with the literal meaning of administration. We propose that "ministering to others" can be a *paradoxical, both-and* phenomenon. We find this proposition compelling because, on the one hand, many definitions refer to leadership as behavior that causes others to *do what they otherwise would* not *do* (for example, Burns, 1978). In other words, we are urged that leadership needs to be strong, decisive, or authoritarian. On the other hand, however, authoritarian behavior is inconsistent with principles of democracy, and it is this inconsistency between authoritarianism and democracy that gives rise to the notion that leadership is paradoxical.

The notion of a "leadership paradox" (Deal & Peterson, 1994) suggests that two fundamentally different ways of viewing and thinking about educational leadership exist. If we are not vigilant, these "two fundamentally different ways" can be needlessly, counterproductively, and impassably separated in leaders' behaviors. The resulting gap, or *gulf,* is interpretable as a consequence of differences in values, beliefs, and cognitive style. For purposes of our discussion of paradox and paradoxical thinking, we posit that "the two different ways" of constructing, interpreting, and managing our worldviews tend to place leaders in one of two conceptual and practical camps. We call these "The Either-or Camp" (TEOC) and "The Both-and Camp" (TBAC).

TEOC (either-or) and TBAC (both-and) provide a useful contrast for thinking about educational leadership. Consider this: Some of us were taught from our earliest moments that what we said, did, and thought was *either* one thing *or* another—what Collins and Porras (1997) call "the tyranny of the or." We were imprinted with the notion that our behaviors were *either* good *or* bad—*either* acceptable *or* unacceptable. According to our nature and nurture, we may be more inclined to support either-or beliefs about the nature of things than both-and (i.e., paradoxical) ideas. In fact, we may be predisposed to resist paradoxical thought and action, or even to deny that our actions reflect philosophical or practical inconsistencies that need to be reconciled.

The American Heritage Dictionary, 2nd ed. (1985, p. 900) tells us that "paradox is a seemingly contradictory statement that may nonetheless be true." Seemingly contradictory, but true. *Both* one thing—*and* something else. *Both* contradictory—*and* true— at the same moment in time (see Hellerstein, 1985). Consider the assertion "Exercise is good and bad." The statement is seemingly contradictory, but nonetheless true. The wrong kind, or too much of the *right* kind of exercise may prove harmful. The *right* kind, in appropriate amounts, can be beneficial.

Many of us have memories of friends or relatives who were *both* kind *and* unkind. We have known a teacher who was *both* wonderfully competent in some ways, *and* woefully incompetent in others. We may have known a child—a student—who was *both* good *and* incorrigible. What, if anything, does the term "love-hate relationship" describe, if not something that is classically and resonantly paradoxical? How many of us have not had a relationship with someone we could neither live with—nor without?

In this chapter, we describe and clarify some of the critical differences between either-or and both-and, or *paradoxical*, thinking. We also point out stumbling blocks that can handicap the efforts of educational leaders who aspire to paradoxical ways of thinking and acting. Most importantly, we show how leadership styles are related to leaders' values and beliefs and provide suggestions and exercises designed to help *develop* paradoxical thought and action.

THINKING ABOUT STYLES

Many of us have more or less conscious preferences about the kinds of people we like to work *with* and the kinds of situations we like to work *in*. People known as random abstract thinkers tend to enjoy others whose thinking also tends to ramble companionably from idea to apparently unrelated idea. Random-abstract individuals often frustrate, and sometimes anger, those who favor concrete-sequential patterns. Random abstracts tend to be comfortable in situations in which boundaries, rules, processes, standards, and expectations may be absent, incomplete, unclear, or fluctuating.

People who are authentically concrete-sequential prefer ordinal, clear, "logical" sequences. They like the order and predictability that accompany association with like-minded others. Concrete-sequentials also tend to prefer organizations that reflect clarity, specificity, and predictable cause-effect relationships in limits, rules, expectations, standards, and structures.

Does any of this suggest that either of the "styles" is essentially or necessarily better or more correct than the other? As one thinks about the question, it becomes apparent that the answer is "yes, *but!*" The qualifying "but" indicates a need for heightened awareness and vigilance regarding situational conditions and requirements within which the choice of style is made. It should be sufficient to point out that in situations involving traumatic life-threatening injury, appropriate decisive action is clearly required—action consistent with what we usually call concrete-sequential behavior. Alternatively, the development of a proposed curriculum for technological literacy is an activity that benefits from a more developmental, nondeterministic approach. "Developmental" connotes taking account of amounts and rates of technological change, for example, in ways that minimize the effects of obsolescence. "Nondeterministic" suggests that prescriptive, close-ended plans should not arbitrarily be imposed in fluid, unpredictable environments. Deterministic, preordained plans are not likely to work when environments change so rapidly that problems also telescope and transform at rates that make *traditional* solutions inappropriate. In other words, the speed and adaptability of problem solving and planning need to complement the dynamic requirements of unique situations.

Four key observations need to be made here:

♦ It is usually helpful and often imperative to be reflectively aware of our leadership styles, tendencies and preferences;

♦ Different situations require leadership approaches that are appropriately adaptable to situational requirements;

♦ The ability to effectively adapt leadership in situationally appropriate ways sometimes requires use of a less-than-preferred approach; and

♦ The ability to effectively adapt less-preferred behaviors requires conceptual and practical flexibility.

WHERE DO I "FIT"?

Students of leadership who are interested in exploring their use of both-and logic and thinking may find some help in the 10 items included in Figure 2.1. The items in the figure are design-

FIGURE 2.1. STYLE TYPE INDICATOR FOR
ASSESSING PREFERRED LOGICAL FORM

1. I tend to learn new things best by:

Browsing the   1   2   3   4   5   6   Reading an
    Internet   assigned text

2. Good supervisors:

Set clear limits   1   2   3   4   5   6   Provide general
                                       guidance*

3. Random-abstract thought is:

Novel and   1   2   3   4   5   6   Unnecessary and
    productive   wasteful

4. Productive questions:

Have one   1   2   3   4   5   6   Have several
    answer   answers*

5. When procedures are unclear, good workers:

Explore   1   2   3   4   5   6   Work deductively

6. Organizational productivity suffers when:

Rules are   1   2   3   4   5   6   Rules are rigid*
    flexible

7. Concrete-sequential thought is:

Deliberate and   1   2   3   4   5   6   Productive
    pedantic

8. The best leaders are those who lead:

Scientifically   1   2   3   4   5   6   Artistically*

9. Life is least satisfying when it is governed by:

Single choices   1   2   3   4   5   6   Multiple
                                       challenges

10. Students should approach new information with:

Silent   1   2   3   4   5   6   Clarifying
    acceptance   questions*

ed to identify *tendencies* to prefer either-or logic and to think in either-or terms, or to prefer both-and logic, and think in both-and, or paradoxical, ways. This "style type indicator" is most useful if some basic points are kept in mind as it is completed: First, you are under no obligation to share your score with anyone. Second, you will get the best indication of your "style" by picking your choices on the scoring scale quickly and candidly.

Scores on the indicator range theoretically from 10 to 60. To evaluate your tendencies to favor membership in TEOC (the either-or camp) or TBAC (the both-and camp), you should first reverse-score items marked with asterisks. That is, convert 6 to 1, 5 to 2, 4 to 3, and so forth. After completing the reverse-scoring procedure, sum the 10 scores. The closer your score is to 10, the more you tend to favor TBAC. The closer to 60, the more you tend to favor TEOC. We also should acknowledge something that will already be apparent to some readers: The closer your score is to the midpoint, 35, the more able you probably already are to behave transactionally—to move with facility from either-or to both-and thinking. This is certainly an important complement of well-developed leadership beliefs and values.

ANALYZING YOUR LOGICAL PREFERENCE

As we have just suggested, preferences for either TEOC-ic or TBAC-ic logic and thought should not be viewed as labels that are arbitrarily, dogmatically, or unchangeably assumed or assigned. Both forms, and their transactional midpoint, are appropriate according to the requirements of different situations. Having said that, we suggest that the value of the information gained from the instrument is maximized by paying close attention to *the strength of tendency evident in your response.* The closer your score was to 60, the stronger your preference is to either-or logic and thought; a score closer to 10 indicates a preference for both-and thinking. Given the evident importance of leaders' abilities to adapt their use of logic—their analytic thought—according to the exigencies of specific situations, the following argument can be made that (a) skilled leaders judge the requirements of specific situations accurately; (b) skilled leaders act, or guide action, in ways that positively affect situational requirements; (c) positive outcomes depend on leaders providing or fa-cilitating logic and analytical thought appropriate to specific sit-uational circumstances; and (d) the ability to provide appropriate logic and thought is influenced extensively by the leader's adaptability and flexibility. It follows that students of leadership who aspire to successful careers must "know them-selves"—their leanings, preferences, tendencies, hang-ups, blind spots, beliefs, and values—and will work reflectively and effectively to become highly skilled in accurate judgment. They will *effectively adapt* their logic and thought in flexible ways to situational requirements.

Does this advice place the student of leadership at some risk of becoming a leader who is viewed by colleagues as indecisive or dysfunctionally suggestible? A realistic, pragmatic answer acknowledges that such a risk most certainly *does* exist. And, to risk compounding what may already be confusing, the environ-ment in which the risk occurs in the first place becomes even *more* complex in light of another paradoxical leadership notion: *Flexible consistency.* Given the existence of risk compounded by paradox, how might the risk be minimized while managing the paradoxical requirement for flexible consistency?

A helpful beginning to the task of risk management can be made by recognizing and understanding how leader *consistency* and leader *success* are related. In our effort to shed light on this important relationship, we first consulted a premier source on the topic, *The Handbook of Leadership* (Bass, 1990). Interestingly, the *Handbook* has relatively little to say about consistency, and what it does say is related primarily to consistency as *transfer-ability*, or leaders' capacities for leading effectively across situa-tions. This source also tends to be male-related in its commen-taries on consistency. Given our interest here in establishing meanings and understandings that may interest and inform both females *and* males, we have turned to formal logic (Carroll, 1977) and conjecture (deJouvenal, 1967) for tools and processes. Consider the statements in Figure 2.2 and decide how you would answer from the choices of always, sometimes, and never.

FIGURE 2.2. LOGICAL ASSERTIONS ABOUT LEADERSHIP

Item	*True*
1. Some successful leaders are consistent:	(Always, Sometimes, Never)
2. Some consistent leaders are successful	(Always, Sometimes, Never)
3. All successful leaders are consistent	(Always, Sometimes, Never)
4. All consistent leaders are successful	(Always, Sometimes, Never)
5. No successful leader is consistent	(Always, Sometimes, Never)
6. No consistent leader is successful	(Always, Sometimes, Never)

Figure 2.1 (p. 33) includes elements that are essential to logical analysis: (a) set, or *class* membership; that is, some, all, or no(ne); (b) attributes of the set or class; that is, success and consistency; and (c) truth value of the claim; that is, always, sometimes, or never true. As the assertions are read in numerical order, it is apparent that the "truth" of each pair of "consistency/success assertions" changes from always to sometimes to never. We can change the statements to include their truth values: "Some successful leaders are always consistent" (1). "All successful leaders are sometimes consistent" (3), and "No successful leader is never consistent" (5).

If we consider how these logical assertions about the relationship of consistency and success in leadership may be interpreted in terms of practical application, we can see the *range of behavioral possibility* that is clearly implied by the logic of the assertions. We know from experience that there are some successful (wise and enlightened) leaders who, for all practical purposes, are always consistent. Almost literally so. We also know from experience or observation that there is almost literally *no* successful leader who is *never* consistent in at least *some* aspect or area of performance—principals who are invariably evenhanded and fair in their treatment of teachers' requests for emergency leave, for example. They are consistent, and teachers understand and support the imperatives that underlie the consistency. When there are exceptions, as there inevitably will be, teachers will understand, accept, and be convinced by the reasoning of successful principals. An illustrative example is apparent in the following anecdote.

A veteran, respected high school mathematics teacher's spouse of forty-plus years is terminally ill. The teacher has exhausted all of his available leave time. The teacher is aware that the principal has uniformly denied all prior requests from teachers for unentitled leave, but he needs one more day of leave before the year's end to take his wife to Central City for chemotherapy. The illness has drained their financial resources, and many of his long-term colleagues have encouraged him to make a "request based on unique, emergency need." The principal in this incident is an experienced, successful, career administrator. The exceptional request was anticipated and, not surprisingly, gave rise to a difficult internal debate on the principal's part. After all, her success was attributable in considerable part to her consistency, and she was fully aware that she had not heretofore granted permission for unentitled leave. Nor had she "winked at" nor turned a blind eye to teachers' use of unauthorized leave. Therefore, it surprised many of the staff and angered others when, in this very special case, the principal....

The ellipses, of course, are deliberate. The decision is left unstated to allow you to address two primary questions. First, what would *you* have done? Why? With what predicted result? Second, is there *a* way, or are there *alternative* ways of *both* serving policy *and* addressing the obvious needs that are unique to this particular situation? Would your action have been more toward the both-and or the either-or end of the continuum? An additional, graphic approach to the technical analysis of the problem is included in Figure 2.3.

FIGURE 2.3. PICKING A HOME ON THE
CONSISTENCY-SUCCESS GRID

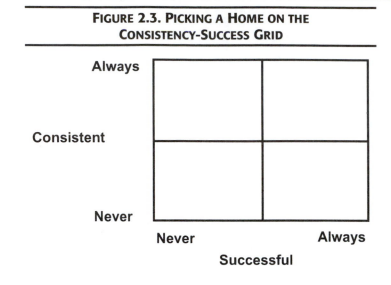

As you begin to think about the place on this grid where you would be best advised to locate, you might recognize that your options will be clarified by addressing some preliminary questions: First, success for whom, determined by what? Second, asking paradoxically, would it be possible to pick a site where *both* consistency *and* success are beneficially and acceptably balanced?

THE CRUCIAL ROLE OF MORALITY AND ETHICS

A convincing answer to the first question needs to be solidly and primarily grounded in reasoned moral principle. Moral and ethical principles should elevate concerns for such things as decency, civility, fairness, justice, freedom, and security to imperative levels. These kinds of concerns should define qualities of school life available to *all* the school's participants. The qualities should be realized in ways that are consistent with what Sergiovanni (1992) calls "covenantal relationships"—relationships that are mutually worked out by participants and treated as binding, in an almost sacred sense. Problem solutions that ignore covenants in order to uniformly and arbitrarily uphold policy threaten to become impoverished. Success, then, is achieved when human activity clearly addresses matters that are morally and ethically imperative. Success should emphatically *not* be associated solely or primarily with impersonal, "objective" outcome measures of academic achievement. To permit that, as Berliner and Biddle (1995) suggest, would be a cruel deception.

SERVING BOTH POLICY AND HUMAN NEEDS

The second question—whether we can serve *both* policy *and* human needs—is even more difficult than "What, why, and with what result?" The increase in difficulty is attributable to concomitant increases in the number of parties involved and affected, the importance and urgency of the issue, and the weight of moral and ethical concern associated with the issue. We need to consider, for example, whether it is true that a single member's need ever obligates the group to support the individual, or is it *always* preferable for an individual to suffer rather than to inconvenience the group? In other words, are there "questions of humanity" involved here that are sufficiently important to warrant discovering or inventing an acceptable path to an exception? Can the situation surrounding the issue be reconstructed in *both-and* fashion? Can you, *should* you, serve *both* the needs of the individual *and* the needs of the group?

We encourage further consideration of a possibility that has already been suggested: The human obligation to treat others decently and compassionately sometimes requires departure from policy and precedent—what might be called a reinvention of policy. In the case of the example, we think it decent and appropriate to deliberately decide and to make appropriate organizational provision for an exception to established precedent and policy. We would not advocate an approach that is devious, confrontive, or procedurally inappropriate—"in violation of policy"—but an exception appears to be warranted "on the face of circumstantial evidence."

MEDIATING DIFFERENCES

Having said that, we recognize that it is appropriate to acknowledge what may be on the minds of many readers: It is always possible for reasonable people to disagree. It is *particularly* possible where a matter of principle is involved. It may be *most* possible when (with a smile): "The *most* reasonable person recognizes what is *obviously* right." The issue of central importance here, we believe, is that questions about what is moral, ethical, principled, or otherwise "right" are inevitably influenced by the subjective values and beliefs of individual participants. Where subjectivity is involved, the appropriateness of answers to questions and solutions to problems tends to be measured with rulers that are somewhat rubbery. In other words, doing what is right, or appropriate, or ethical, or moral in human organizations involves negotiation that is more or less detailed and lengthy depending on the importance of the issue and the strength of subjective perception that separates various preferences. The words used to describe the qualitative characteristics of possible outcomes are themselves "soft and *subj*ective" rather than "hard and *obj*ective." Life-shaping decisions in schools, then, should be recognized as phenomena that are not always amenable to objective, precise, scientific specification and solution. These observations suggest certain things relative to where we may attempt to "live" on the consistency-success grid (Figure 2.3, p. 38).

EXPLORING THE GRID

If you've reviewed and thought about the grid, you've probably already concluded that you would be ill advised to homestead never-never land. That lower-left quadrant is a leadership desert. To aspiring leaders who stay there too long, we might say what the ancient mapmakers said of *terra incognito*—"There be Dragons!"

If we read the grid's ordinate from bottom to top, we see the never-always quadrant of success and consistency: Never successful, always consistent. Like never-never land, the upper-left never-always quad also reveals itself as threatening territory. It may not be uninhabitable, but organizations and their leaders who find themselves scouting that territory would be well advised to explore further east. The northwest will become predictably dull, routine, pedantic, and lifeless.

Reading the abscissa left to right takes us to the never-always quadrant of consistency and success: Never consistent, always successful. Living there is at least theoretically possible, but does it appear to be conducive to sustainable occupancy? We can probably agree that covenantal school life would be improbable in the southeast quadrant. Covenants depend on mutually derived, thoughtfully maintained agreements that are binding. A principal who is never consistent but always successful conjures up the image of a ringmaster leading a parade of clowns: unpredictable, obediently following the whistle, falling all over themselves, now a laugh, now a tragedy. Appropriate to a circus, perhaps, but not to a school.

This leaves only the upper-right, always-always quad. While this one is theoretically possible and obviously the most highly desirable of the four, it also is apparent that very few present or aspiring principals can realistically expect to be *both* consistent *and* right all the time. This probably is not a realistic expectation for even the *most adaptive* thinkers and actors. Practical limitations notwithstanding, it nevertheless seems advisable for aspiring paradoxical thinkers to establish a base camp somewhere near the southwest corner of the northeast (always-always) quadrant. From a base camp in the southwest, a series of trails can be established that terminate around the perimeter of the quadrant from due north to due east. By thinking effectively about where and when you and your colleagues need to "be" on a certain trail under specific circumstances, you will maximize the practical probabilities of achieving the kinds of both-and thought and action essential to survival and success in a paradoxical world. This *is* realistic, because it maximizes the *possibility* of high levels of consistency and success while recognizing that they will not and should not always be equivalent.

PARADOX SPOTTING

The educational leader's ability to effectively use both-and thinking depends on the ability to recognize actual or potential paradoxical situations. We say actual or potential because some situations are *prima facie* candidates for both-and treatment while others are tacitly so. Figure 2.4 includes selected "paradoxical pairs," which provide examples of the kinds of seeming contradictions that successful, contemporary principals have to reconcile.

FIGURE 2.4. EXAMPLES OF PARADOX

Things that are:

Both	*And*
Competitive	Cooperative
Win-Lose Conflict	Win-Win Conflict
Change Agent	Outcome Critic
Equal Opportunity	Meritocratic
Miniature	Giant
More Responsible	Less Influential
Oxymoronic	Logical

An overview of the paradoxical pairs included in Figure 2.4 suggests ways of including the pairs in sentences, which make their paradoxical nature more apparent. In the case of competitive-cooperative, a concerned parent might expect that: "My child must be prepared to be competitive in a global economy, but I insist that all my child's classmates be cooperative in their dealings with him." Where conflict is involved, the possibilities for defining it in more of a win-win than win-lose way depends heavily on the nature of the issue, feelings and beliefs of parties, and skills of the mediator. If it is assumed from the outset that there *must* be a winner and a loser, that assumption obviously will reduce the possibility of discovering or inventing ways of creating multiple winners. Recognition of the frequent possibility of win-win outcomes, however, will keep the both-and principal alert to ways of achieving them. Situations that have the potential to become *either* win-lose *or* win-win can often be transformed into win-win according to their conceptual and practical treatment. What you *see* often is literally what you *get* (see Fisher, Ury, & Patton, 1991).

The paradox of persons or agencies who are *both* agents of change *and* critics of outcomes provides a particular challenge for the contemporary principal. A striking example is evident in Berliner and Biddle's (1995) book, *Manufactured Crisis*. They describe a "crisis" led by "identifiable critics" for reasons which were political (see p. 4): "[M]ost of the claims of the Manufactured Crisis are, indeed, myths, half-truths, and sometimes outright lies." We have had, then, a dozen or so years of continued exhortation for educational reform from identifiable critics, the bases of which have been mythical, half-true, or false. The futility of efforts to "reform" an institution based on a flawed foundation of criticism is obvious, and the relatively uninterrupted flow of criticism of failed reforms should not be surprising. The magnitude of challenge presented for principals by this paradox is significant. One thing seems fairly clear: Successful contemporary principals will need to become well versed in the facts of the matter if they are to have a reasonable hope for formulating an effective strategic response. Command of the varieties of truth and the ability to articulate them effectively are essential elements of both-and skill.

The remaining pairs are not much less challenging. Our culture tacitly recognizes the importance of equality of educational opportunity while insisting that recognition and reward be based on merit. The "miniature giant" paradox may be somewhat obscure, but if we reflect on the enormous influence exerted by the microprocessor in our culture, we quickly get the point. The point is reinforced by Roszak (1994): "While the computer was shrinking...it was taking on a new, disembodied, electronic 'size' that dwarfed all previous technology in the scope of its power" (p. 15)—a miniature giant.

Our schools are being held increasingly responsible for student achievement by the same critics who threaten the schools' very existence. And, interestingly, we uncritically accept the pointed foolishness of oxymorons like "quality control" while at least suspecting that "quality" is a phenomenon which is inherently antagonistic to being "controlled" (see Deming, 1994).

Principals who think and act paradoxically should eventually come round to the realization that democracy itself is much more than a ritualistic label. Democracy is *the* word used to describe a singular cultural institution. That institution, as we know, is one in which all are created equal, endowed with certain unalienable rights, and entitled to life, liberty, and the pursuit of happiness. It should therefore be recognized as an institution in which liberty plays a central role. It also should be recognized as a system in which participants do things because they are convinced they are right—not because they are coerced to do them.

SUMMARY

In this chapter on paradox and paradoxical thinking, we encourage aspiring and practicing principals to reflect on two fundamentally different ways of viewing problems and applying logic to their solutions. Specifically, *either-or* and *both-and* forms of conceptualizing and solving problems were considered. Given the tendencies for many aspects of human existence to *be* paradoxical and the attendant advantages of addressing the problems of human existence through applications of paradoxical logic (Deal & Peterson, 1994; Collins & Porras, 1997; Hellerstein, 1985), approaches to assessing and developing paradoxical leadership approaches were addressed.

ACTION FOLLOW-UP

Develop a statement describing the kind of thinking—both-and or either-or—you hope to use as the primary approach to decision making in your school. Your statement should include a rationale that addresses the kinds of outcome your choice would achieve and why those outcomes are valued.

♦ Share your statement with a partner. Seek constructive feedback on your statement and explain whether and how you would use the feedback to modify your statement. Give special attention to justifying your reasons for not using any suggestions provided.

- In a small discussion group, possibly colleagues identified in the action follow-up for Chapter 1, identify circumstances, conditions, or factors that would pose difficulties for the successful achievement of outcomes described in your statement. Once these challenges are identified, describe and assess possible approaches to overcoming them.

- In the same discussion group, address this question: What are some of the major drawbacks of attempting to take an all-or-nothing approach to the application of both-and or either-or ways of thinking, and how are those drawbacks overcome?

3

ARE YOUR VALUES, BELIEFS, AND ACTIONS CONSISTENT WITH DEMOCRATIC PRINCIPLES?

How do principals maintain consistency among their values, beliefs, behaviors, and democratic principles? Consistency depends in great part on the ability, first, to recognize and then to act in accord with principles of the sort contained in the opening sentences of *The Declaration of Independence*:

> When, in the course of human events, it becomes necessary for one people to dissolve the political bands which have connected them with another, and to assume, among the powers of the earth, the separate and equal station to which the laws of nature and of nature's God entitle them, a decent respect to the opinions of mankind requires that they should declare the causes which impel them to the separation.

> We hold these truths to be self-evident, that all men are created equal; that they are endowed by their Creator with certain unalienable rights; that among these are life, liberty, and the pursuit of happiness. That to secure these rights, governments are instituted among men, deriving their just powers from the consent of the governed; that, whenever any form

of government becomes destructive of these ends, it is the right of the people to alter or to abolish it, and to institute a new government, laying its foundation on such principles, and organizing its powers in such form, as to them shall seem most likely to effect their safety and happiness.

Jefferson asserts that people take certain actions because they are necessary and that certain things are obvious or self-evident. Among these is the need to assume a separate, equal station to which they are entitled. And because it is the right, decent, civil thing to do, when they exercise rights of this sort, people should explain their actions to others. Also note that when "any form of government" becomes tyrannical or otherwise "becomes destructive" of the ends implied by "unalienable rights," *the people have the right to reshape it!* These assertions have the effect and weight of axioms. They include not so much as a scintilla of evidence of negotiability. The Declaration of Independence makes the essential principles of democracy plain:

The inherent worth of one individual is equal to the worth of any other individual. All people are entitled to life, liberty, and the pursuit of happiness. Every participant in a democratically organized institution is entitled to have a voice in the governance of that institution. The enjoyment of freedom is qualified by requirements to assume related responsibilities and obligations. In democratically formed institutions the exercise of authority is qualified and constrained, among other things, by the individual's right to due process. The power to govern resides with the people.

Principles of this sort are susceptible to being imperfectly understood and applied. While commitment to democracy is espoused, undemocratic habits and expectations legitimize undemocratic structures and practices and make the achievement of democracy incomplete. If anyone should doubt this, reflect on acts that cause people to experience discrimination. Individuals and groups become targets of discrimination for a variety of uncivil reasons. These reasons include differential treatment of members of groups who are identifiable, for example, by race, ethnicity, wealth, class, gender, and belief system. Under certain circumstances, the defining sociological and biological attributes of an individual or group are sufficient to attract extraordinarily positive or negative treatment. Diffident adolescent males are bullied by more confident agemates. Athletic, ebullient female adolescents are counseled to not be too boy-like. Racially identifiable children and youth are subjected to slurs.

Anecdotes abound in which building administrators are threatened with inappropriate sanctions by district administrators. As the abstract, conceptual problem of integrating beliefs, values, and behaviors is contemplated, it is important to consider the concrete, practical issue of responding when a superior calls and says: "I hear you've disciplined Rob Jones. You obviously don't know this, but Rob's dad is a close friend of mine. He's upset by your action. You need to understand something. You could lose your job if you don't revoke the penalty." Experiences of this sort teach invaluable lessons. If a superior directs you to rescind a fairly administered penalty as "a favor to a friend," it should be apparent that you are being required to extend an unearned privilege or to assign an undeserved status which is a function of a special relationship—not because it is the right, democratic thing to do. What are your options?

You can comply with the directive and rationalize your action by reminding yourself (a) the requester is your superior; (b) you're just following orders; (c) you have no alternative; (d) you can't afford to be insubordinate; and, most importantly, (e) you can't afford to lose your job. Alternately, you might choose to ignore the directive and hope that your insubordination will go undetected. But you would probably conclude—correctly—that Rob's father and your superior would continue communicating with the predictable result that your neglect will be noticed. At least one alternative remains. It requires you to first recognize that your superior's behavior is unprofessional and undemocratic. Having recognized the inappropriateness of your superior's behavior, you should assess your ability to refuse to comply and the consequences of refusing.

Your assessment should take note of several things. How do your personal and positional powers compare with your supe-

rior's powers? Assuming that your answer to is "not very favor-
ably," you then ask whether you can either recruit help from the
principal, superintendent, or some other potential supporter
who will secure your ability to refuse. As you are evaluating the
short-term strategy, you also should keep in mind the importance of assessing longer-term consequences. Prominent among
these should be concern about your ability to *both* serve democracy *and* survive. In other words, knowing that your philosophical commitment to fairness and justice will have consequences
that may be physical, negative, and personal, will your commitment, conviction, and courage be sufficient to carry you through
difficult future relationships with your superior and Rob's father? Knowing that virtues can be lost if they are treated indif-
ferently, it is important to reflect on the extent to which you will
act in their service. If you take seriously the suggestion to examine your zeal for defending virtue, it will probably occur to you
to ask just how self-sacrificial one has to be in defense of virtue
in order to qualify as an acceptable moral agent. Is it necessary,
for example, to be an active, energetic supporter of the general
welfare, or is it sufficient to avoid doing wrong to others?

> Most nonutilitarian philosophers...believe that we
> have some obligation to promote the general welfare,
> but they typically view this obligation as less strin-
> gent than, for example, the obligation not to injure
> people. They see us as having a much stronger obli-
> gation to refrain from violating people's rights than
> to promote their happiness or well being (Shaw, 1993,
> p. 29).

Your reflection on issues of this sort may lead to helpful in-
sights about your commitment to democracy, your character, integrity, courage, and willingness to compromise or betray those
things in the service of self-interest.

The possibility that disagreement can result from attempts
to democratize schools provides an additional incentive for you
principals to be well grounded in your beliefs. In saying this, we
are suggesting that your beliefs should not be so fragile, superfi-
cial, and unintegrated that they can be easily and successfully
attacked by determined critics. A potentially useful approach to

the formulation of well-conceived, effectively integrated, and defensible beliefs relies on disclosing and discussing them. Disclosing and discussing philosophical beliefs and values can be threatening, but the value of a compelling commitment to democracy makes the risks of self-scrutiny bearable. Certain ground rules may help to minimize threat and discomfort.

- ♦ Agree on an order in which individual participants will state beliefs and values.

- ♦ Agree that it's okay for anyone to "pass" until they're ready to participate.

- ♦ Agree that you will paraphrase a person's statement of belief or value to their satisfaction before commenting on it.

- ♦ Agree that you will limit your comments and criticisms to the *content of beliefs and values*—not to the motivations or character of the originator. In other words, agree that you will not engage in an *ad hominem* criticism or attack.

What follow in the chapter are suggestions for assessing the consistency of your values and beliefs with democratic principle, approaches to appraising schools for their consistency with democratic organization and practice, and discussion of strategies and techniques for transforming schools into places where democracy is not only studied, but lived.

HOW DEMOCRATIC AM I?

Predispositions or tendencies to act democratically are effects of multiple causes, which are inherently and heavily value-laden and value-dependent. Why does one deal fairly with others? Why place a lost-and-found notice when we find valuables that do not belong to us? Why defend the defenseless, protect the weak, feed the hungry, or do any manner of good with no particular expectation of recognition or reward?

Some actions in the service of democracy grow out of rational conclusions that acting democratically advances human welfare and therefore makes obvious sense. Since democracy serves the general human condition, it will ultimately be better if all individuals choose to act democratically. The notion is similar to the idea that a rising tide lifts all boats. Other democratic actions are caused by deep impressions made during formative years by nurturing, influential relatives and friends. While some act democratically in their youth because it is expected or required, it is also true that those youthful acts of compliance sometimes ripen into acts of conviction in the mature adult.

Acting in consistently democratic ways requires what Jefferson and certain of his contemporaries recognized: the ability to discern democratic principles and distinguish them from others that are not. This critical ability to discern and distinguish depends on knowing what a principle is. In making an attempt to know what a principle is, we can probably do no better than rely on lexical sources. These tell us that principles are basic truths, laws, or assumptions; rules; or standards—especially *of good behavior* (*American Heritage Dictionary, 2nd ed.,* 1985, p. 985). Shaw (1993) provides a more finely grained understanding of "principle" in referring to it as a rule "that people in effect formulate in determining their conduct" (p. 24). At this point, someone will surely want to know how distinctions are made between good behavior and not good behavior. Our choice of answer is found in Jefferson's words: Good behavior, we would argue, is the kind which, regularly applied by and to people, "shall seem most likely to effect their Safety and Happiness" (Jefferson, 1776).

Once we learn to recognize democratic, principled, good behavior, then if we wish or intend to act democratically it is necessary to acquire and integrate attitudes, beliefs, values, predispositions, and *other* attributes associated with democratic action. If you ask why one *should* act democratically, we will repeat what we have already suggested: Democracy places people first and is therefore the moral, ethical, civil, principled, *right* way to act. If you ask whether there are not instances and situations wherein concern for self-interest dictates acting in ways that are undemocratic, we would acknowledge that there are. Any of several variations on "survival games" will quickly demonstrate that self-preservation is sometimes secured at another's expense. You and another person are marooned on an island. You have enough food to sustain the two of you for one week. Rescue will not arrive before two weeks have elapsed. If either of you is to survive, one of you must not. It is not our purpose here to moralize about selfishness, self-preservation, self-sacrifice, or the appropriateness of suicide or murder. It is, rather, to encourage you to wonder whether a person who ultimately is committed to self-preservation can claim to be committed to democracy. Because self-preservation is ultimately a zero-sum, winner-take-all proposition, democratic concern for "we the people" rather than "I the individual" is an arguably attractive proposition.

Some of us work within frameworks of belief that assume that one or more leaders that are heroic are necessary for the achievement of democratic purpose. We read and hear assertions to the effect that visionary leadership or some equally superlative form of it is essential to the recovery and perpetuation of democracy. Interestingly, Sergiovanni (1992) cites Kant's second categorical imperative ("Act so that you treat humanity, whether in your own person or in that of another, always as an end and never as a means only." Kant, Immanuel (1959). *Foundations of the Metaphysics of Morals.* (Trans. L.W. Beck.) New York: Bobbs-Merrill. (Originally published 1785)) with approval, and then observes,

> Were this rule to reign in the world of leadership, much of the existing literature on the topic (based on the purpose of leadership as getting others to do what the leader wants and like it in the bargain) would need to be scrapped. Leaders would still exert influence and try to make things happen, but the authority for what they do would not be the clever use of psychological skills; it would be the substance of ideas, values, and commitments. Leaders would have to be more open in their intentions and more forthright in their means (p. 106).

We agree with Sergiovanni's assertion, and think the analysis might be extended to address the issue of leadership in democratic contexts. Consider, for example, how commonplace it has become to read or to hear "the leader" whenever organizational effectiveness or improvement is being considered. In fact, give yourself a simple test. Read the following assertion and then reflect on your reaction:

> *Visionary leadership is an imperative element in an effective school.*

Did you have any noticeable reaction? Did you think, "Sure, that's right!" Did you think, perhaps, that the assertion is fundamentally correct, but really needs to acknowledge that the visionary leadership is expected to come *from the principal* if the school is to be *really* effective? Well and good. Consider the following:

> We, the people of the United States, in order to form a more perfect union, establish justice, insure domestic tranquility, provide for the common defense, promote the general welfare, and secure the blessings of liberty to ourselves and our posterity, do ordain and establish this Constitution for the United States of America.

How do the two beginnings differ—*the leader,* and *we, the people?* We are inclined to think they are worlds apart. Emphasis on "the leader" immediately induces an expectation that status differences will inevitably or necessarily exist, as they are conventionally assumed to exist between leader and led. One will be set apart in a hierarchically superior position. Consequently, we will expect to have "the leader" telling the rest of us what to think and how, otherwise, to act. But the preamble to the Constitution relies on "we, the people." It becomes an interesting and challenging matter to speculate about how principals whose values and beliefs are grounded in "we, the people" assumptions would compare with principals who assume "the leader" to be a necessary ingredient of success. That is not, of course, to say that *influence* of some sort is not essential to the shaping of group effort.

In the following list are items designed to help you assess the "goodness of fit" among values you think you subscribe to, beliefs you claim to hold, and their alignment, respectively, with each other. Prior to talking about them with colleagues, it would be worthwhile to clarify what it is, specifically, that you'll be thinking about and discussing.

Are My Values and Beliefs Consistent?

♦ Can I value democracy and deny students due process?

♦ Can my school teach democracy without being organized and operated democratically?

♦ Can I be a democratic principal if I fail to maintain the confidence of students, faculty and patrons?

♦ Does being a democratic principal mean that I'll never make a "big decision" unilaterally?

♦ If my school has several student groups that are identifiable by certain characteristics, should those groups be proportionally represented on school teams, performing groups, and activities?

♦ If I were really democratic, would I become a principal?

For purposes of our list, we've taken "value" to mean "a principle, standard, or quality considered worthwhile or desirable" (*The American Heritage Dictionary, 2nd ed.*, 1985, p. 1336). Notice that the definition refers to "principle," a term we've already encountered, a word that connotes truths, laws, rules, or standards. Values and principles, then, are closely linked as to meaning. They are aggressively and robustly qualitative terms, referring as they do to abstract, intangible, but nevertheless essential ingredients of purposeful living. We might do better to talk in terms that are more literal about values as we attempt to get our heads wrapped around an effective understanding of them.

Think for a moment about some questions: Is that thing valuable? In other words, is it something that has worth? Does kindness have value? Does consideration have value? Does selfishness have value? Should we be encouraged to think in ways that recognize gradations of worth among *competing* values, which are influenced or conditioned—"caused," in a certain sense—by subjective preference and situational features?

Should we cling to a dogmatic posture that holds certain values to be universal and absolute? The careful reader will note, of course, that close examination of questions of this sort can lead quickly and frustratingly to contradictions and unsolvable puzzles. For example, consider the assertion: "All values are subject to modification according to particular requirements of specific situations." That seems perfectly reasonable—synonymous with: "All values are relative," right? But wait a minute! The assertion, "All values are relative" is an absolute. It contradicts itself! You might take this as a reminder to be on the lookout for logical contradictions as you ponder your "consistencies."

Belief, according to our source, entails placing confidence in a person or thing. An important distinction can be made, then, between values—standards, law-like statements of worth—and beliefs or the confidence we *place* in certain standards. The difference can be emphasized by thinking about a *standard for truthfulness* (e.g., it is always/usually important to be truthful) and *beliefs about truthfulness* (e.g., so-and-so is telling the truth, or so-and-so is known to be truthful, so I believe so-and-so's statement is true). As we think about it in greater detail, we can see that we're concerned about a triangle-like arrangement of things: values, beliefs, democratic principles. The first and third members of this set—values and democratic principles—are perhaps the most closely related, but not synonymously or redundantly, of course, because not all values are democratic. The above questions are intended to help you examine the relationships among your values, beliefs, and commitment to democratic principle. While there may not be answers that are absolutely right or wrong, we think there are some that are better than others. You'll find our thoughts about that at the end of the chapter. Try to avoid looking ahead. Discuss the questions with one or two colleagues.

HOW DEMOCRATIC IS MY SCHOOL?

It is our hope that you reflect with special rigor on the idea of democracy as you read this section. We are encouraged to express that hope by believing or having confidence in the proposition that democracy is based on values which are demonstrably worthy in terms of their good effects on human existence. Some particularly noteworthy examples of these values are provided by the following assertions:

+ All of human life is inherently valuable.

+ All humans have certain entitlements or rights.

+ All of human life owes certain obligations—has duties—to others.

Two things should be highlighted as you think about these assertions. First, they are themselves based or grounded on certain values. One of the most essential of these grounding values is the concept of unconditional, unqualified—unalienable—rights. In the particular case of schools, it is appropriate to think of students, staff, and patrons as persons entitled without qualification to respectful treatment. If you effectively commit yourselves as principals and assistant principals to treating others respectfully, it is probable that your moral choice will have positive results. Similarly, as your values and beliefs develop in morally influential ways, you will find them contributing in increasingly valuable ways to your school's culture.

Second, as you reflect further on our three assertions, notice that they've been stated in a way that's consistent with the manner of Kant's categorical imperative; that is, they "command unconditionally" (Shaw, 1993, p. 25). It will aid your cultivation of a personal moral philosophy if you take the "imperative nature" of our three assertions as an invitation to refute them. In order to attempt this, you need to know that the substance of Kant's categorical imperative holds that right moral acts must be capable of becoming universal laws of conduct. Furthermore, if an assertion about right moral action contradicts itself, it cannot become universal and hence cannot qualify as a categorical imperative. Dewey (1910) says the Greeks tried to find a rational basis for ethical theory rather than continuing to rely on custom.

> But reason as a substitute for custom was under the obligation of supplying objects and laws as fixed as those of custom had been. Ethical theory ever since has been singularly hypnotized by the notion that its business is to discover some final end or good or

some ultimate and supreme law…there was one point in which they were agreed: a single and final source of law (pp. 493–494).

Dewey also expresses regret that scientific method—what he refers to as "intellectual reconstruction"—had not been used effectively "in the moral and social disciplines" (p. 494).

After all, then, we are only pleading for the adoption in moral reflection of the logic that has been proved to make for security, stringency and fertility in passing judgment upon physical phenomena (p. 495).

Much of the discussion of values by philosophers prior to the postmodern era emphasized the role and importance of rationality in making choices among competing values. The argument runs something like this: Because preferred value choices are derivable from well-applied reason, and because humans are thinking beings, it follows that human reason should be applied in making value choices. But then we have Simon's (1957) assertion: "There is no way in which the correctness of ethical propositions can be empirically or rationally tested" (p. 47). In other words, Simon is positing that rationality cannot be applied to questions of right and wrong. Dewey supports the application of reason to questions of value, Simon argues against it. At the risk of increasing the confusion, let us turn for a moment to the central principle addressed in a classic essay on the human condition. *On Liberty,* by John Stuart Mill (1859) (in Rader & Gill, 1991), begins with Mill's assertion that there is just one principle "entitled to govern absolutely the dealings of society with the individual" (p. 586).

That principle is, that the sole end for which mankind are warranted, individually or collectively, in interfering with the liberty of action of any of their number, is self-protection. That the only purpose for which power can be rightfully exercised over any member of a civilized community, against his will, is to prevent harm to others.…Over himself, over his own body and mind, the individual is sovereign (p. 586).

So we learn from our examples that we *should* use our reasoning abilities in making values choices—in establishing our philosophical values and beliefs; that we *cannot* apply rational processes to ethical questions, thus making the issue of whether we should or not moot; and that only one principle is entitled to "govern absolutely" our social relationships—each of us is entitled to liberty *unless* our exercise of that right interferes with others' liberty.

Many of you will have noted that values tend by nature to be controversial, characterized as they so often are by features that are not amenable to objective, definitive scrutiny. Simon appears to have gotten this part of it right. But do you think it follows from this, as Simon did, that we should ignore ethical aspects of questions if we are to have any realistic hope of developing a science of administration? We think Dewey would probably say no. In either case, you should anticipate serious challenges when setting out to explore these kinds of issues in your school. We need do no more to be convinced of this than remember the numbers of people who argue in good faith that questions of human reason and individual liberty are at all times irrelevant because all answers come from God. As we ponder this, we would also do well to remember that the First Amendment to the Constitution of the United States clearly and explicitly states that government will neither establish a religion nor prohibit the practice of religion. This attention to the separation of the powers of government and the church is a reflection, of course, of a desire to protect the sovereignty of "the people"—to shelter them from religious oppression of the kind the early English colonists fled. It seems to be consistent with a requirement that schools—at least public schools—should effectively strive to operate within frameworks of organization and procedure that reflect democratic intent. Having said this, of course, we must acknowledge the potential confusion characterized by much of our currency and coinage being inscribed with "In God We Trust."

Let us return to a consideration of the three focal questions: Is all of human life *inherently* valuable? Do *all* people have certain rights? Do *all* of us owe others certain obligations? Would you argue that life, at least as a value, is miraculous and precious, or would you prefer to take a more deterministic view—life is really not much of anything unless and until personal action and circumstance give it shape and substance? Or further, would you prefer not to be boxed in to either of these alternatives? Would you rather argue that life is really *both* miraculous *and* deterministic?

Where do you prefer to be on these questions and why? They have obvious capacities to challenge and frustrate. More importantly, they have profound capacities for giving shape and direction to human relationships. Given the crucial influence exerted by questions of value and the apparent ease with which students, patrons, and staff fall into rancorous disagreement over value-laden issues, it seems essential for principals to be thoughtfully grounded in their beliefs and compelling in their abilities to articulate them. Pick a discussion partner or form groups of four to share and challenge your answers to the focus questions. Following that, review the questions below and see whether you can develop answers that are compelling, defensible, and consistent with democratic principle.

How Democratic Is My School If...

- Students and staff are not involved in developing rules and procedures?
- Students and staff are involved in developing rules and procedures, but only those that I deem important to them?
- Students and patrons feel uncomfortable sharing concerns and ideas with staff, including me?
- Certain kids get called on and picked for special activities at noticeably higher rates than other kids?
- Any time staff want something to happen, they know they can send a certain colleague to see me and it will?
- It's usually the last school in the district to be repaired, receive new equipment, and so forth?
- I unilaterally decide which teachers get the new computers?

♦ I work with the juvenile division at our local police department to develop a new system for addressing gang-related problems and announce it to staff and parents?

♦ Everyone thinks it's kind of cute that we have kids wear toilet seats around their necks as restroom passes?

♦ If a kid breaks a rule, we "nail 'em"? None of that due process monkey business around here!

♦ We offer a course called "Street Law" and at a certain point the students begin serving as jurors in peer offense hearings?

♦ Freshmen who step on the mascot seal in the front entrance get "noogied" by upperclassmen?

♦ Parents believe I dance to the tune played by our PTO officers?

♦ Kids and staff understand that we operate on merit in our school. If they work hard—and successfully —they get opportunities?

SOME IDEAS ON MAKING SCHOOLS MORE DEMOCRATIC

A brief glance at Figure 1.1 (p. 7) will provide a helpful reminder that change, if it is to be anything other than arbitrarily imposed, begins with a necessary recognition that opportunities exist to improve the *status quo*. When this recognition emerges in its most organizationally helpful way, it usually takes the form of some individual recognizing that a better way of doing things exists. This individual may be the principal, but it is not necessary that this be the case. What *is* necessary to organic, potentially long-lived improvement is a realistic prospect that: (a) what is proposed is desirable; (b) what is proposed is achievable; and (c) what is proposed is sustainable.

Does this suggest that proposals for making a given school more democratic must be unanimously embraced if they are to have reasonable chances of succeeding? We do not think so. You'll remember from discussion in Chapter 1 that democratic procedure does not require that everyone get his or her way. It *does* require everyone's interests to be fairly considered and everyone to have fair influence on decisions. In thoughtfully planned approaches to making schools more democratic, understandings about how decisions will be made are wisely established early in the process and care is taken to ensure that they are democratic.

Why make schools more democratic? An apparent argument for increasing democratic process and practice in schools stems from the belief that *schools have an obligation to teach democracy. They do that most effectively when they are organized and operated democratically.* Does that mean that democratically oriented schools will be chaotic, inherently disorderly places? Again, we think not. Remember that our democratic republic has laws that citizens are to abide by. Remember, too, that those of us who *fail* to abide by our laws are *subject* to sanctions. We have emphasized *subject* as a way of acknowledging that not *all* lawbreakers are caught and, when they are, they are not *always* subjected to what are universally recognized as just penalties. We would argue, however, that recognized flaws and failings of democracy are not persuasive, as values, for considering the abandonment of democracy's ideals.

Initiatives to make schools more democratic can be undertaken as features of existing improvement plans that exist in contemporary schools. *If* a school's site council or building-level improvement team agree that it is important for the school to model democracy more effectively, that intent can be articulated as a goal in the improvement plan. Once this critical step is taken, the initiative may be pursued in much the same way other desirable improvements are undertaken. A subcommittee might be established whose work will include specifying attributes of a democratically organized school, current practices that are inconsistent with those attributes, and plans for selecting practices that will be targeted for improvement. The details of task, process, responsibility, time, and assessment can be handled in established ways. The important, difficult issue, it seems to us, is establishing a firm, effective commitment to the idea that schools should be more effective instruments for the service of democracy. As an ideal, it seems to be entirely consistent with the sort of thing that makes some schools extraordinarily effective and meritorious. The key seems to lie in the establishment of a value and belief that commits a school to becoming as democratic as it can.

ARE MY VALUES AND BELIEFS CONSISTENT?

Earlier in the chapter, we promised to share our thinking on the questions provided to guide the development of answers to the consistency question. Because this section addresses the challenges of making schools more democratic, it is fitting to provide answers and relate them to the school democratization process. We address the questions briefly, in their original order.

- ◆ Can I value democracy and deny students due process?

  The *really* short answer is no. To elaborate just a bit, we believe schools in democratic cultures serve those cultures best when they model the culture's ideals. Because due process is an important feature of the Constitution of the United States (see Amendments 5 and 14), the schools should exemplify that constitutional guarantee. That is not to say that "the process due" students, staff, and others related to schools should ever be so elaborate that its administration places others at risk. In other words, in an instance where a student has injured someone and threatens to do so again if not appropriately constrained, due process procedures should be adjusted to provide appropriate safeguards against further injuries. Practices in this area must be well informed by knowledge of special requirements that apply to mandated due process procedures for special needs students (Fischer, Schimmel, & Kelly, 1999), but due process should be afforded to *all*.

- ◆ Can my school teach democracy without being organized and operated democratically?

  If socialization to the rights and duties of citizenship are *not* taught by and exemplified in schools and school practices, why should educators object if their students accuse them of hypocrisy? Democratic organization and operation does not necessarily imply disorder or other things we would not associate with effective, appropriate schooling. Democratic organization and practice *might* entail changing the way things are done, and these kinds of change might sometimes be, or appear to be, inefficient. We think the benefits of having students experience democracy in their schools justifies the kinds of inconvenience that might result. The benefits are worth the costs.

♦ Can I be a democratic principal if I fail to maintain the confidence of students, faculty, and patrons?

We believe the answer is no. The answer demands qualification, of course. A momentary setback in relations with students, staff, and patrons is not necessarily synonymous with a need to find a new job. Where confidence is lacking over extended periods of time, however, it will be difficult to lead effectively. Lack of confidence is often associated with perceived unfairness, indecisiveness, arbitrariness, or other attributes associated with lack of competence. Where confidence is chronically lacking, principals will find it extremely difficult to be effective in *any* attempted style—autocratic, bureaucratic, *or* democratic.

♦ Does being a democratic principal mean that I'll never make a "big decision" unilaterally?

No. In fact, *failure* to act unilaterally and *decisively* when the combined importance and urgency of a given situation demand it may have consequences so severe that serious injury, permanent impairment, or fatalities result. When you see arterial blood spurting from a wound, you do not form a committee to study emergency medical procedures.

♦ If my school has several student groups that are identifiable by certain characteristics, should those groups be proportionally represented on school teams, in performing groups, and activities?

Not necessarily, although this is an area that gives rise to rancorous values conflicts. Our thinking on the question is that democracy most definitely requires certain things—life, liberty, the *pursuit* of happiness, and equal *opportunity*. Remember what Strike, Haller, and Soltis (1988) said: "A decision is made democratically if: (1) The interests of each individual are fairly considered. (2) Each individual has a fair influence on the decision" (p. 94). While we are endowed by our Creator with certain unalienable rights, we are not all endowed with the same aptitudes and abilities. A school *might* democratically decide that the costs of selective participation are so high as to warrant not *having* them—competitive sport teams, performing groups, and so forth, as some middle schools do not. If we democratically elect to *have* them, however, our schools need to teach that the opportunity to *try* to participate must sometimes suffice.

♦ If I were really democratic, would I become a principal?

We think that so long as schools elect to have principals, it is *especially* desirable that people with strong commitments to democracy and democratic practice should aspire to the role. The evidence for the preference is almost self-evident. If schools are to become more democratic, that achievement is much more likely to be influenced by principals with democratic leanings than by principals who are something other than democratically oriented.

SUMMARY

This chapter addressed the issue of consistency among values, beliefs, actions, and democratic principles. Our thesis is that attributes of any one of these things—values, beliefs, actions, and democratic principles—that are inconsistent with attributes of the others will lead to contradictions which ultimately make our school a less effective and desirable place than it is capable of being. The chapter included suggestions for evaluating the consistency of values and beliefs with democratic principle, described some approaches to assessing the consistency of schools' organization and practice with democracy, and discussed ways of making schools living laboratories for democracy.

ACTION FOLLOW-UP

♦ With a partner, develop a statement describing how a school would function if: (a) The principal operated from a values/beliefs system that began with, "As principal, I must always assure that..." or (b) "In our school, the staff, students, and parents must always be satisfied that...." As you think about this follow-up exercise, be sure to note its similarity to "the leader" and "we, the people."

♦ Evaluate Simon's assertion that "there is no way in which the correctness of ethical propositions can be empirically or rationally tested." As you complete your evaluation, you might consider various examples of ethical propositions and ask whether their correctness cannot, in fact, be tested empirically or rationally. One example of such a proposition for your consideration is: "Ethical propositions have no influence on the amount and quality of fairness and justice evident in human affairs."

♦ Many, if not most, contemporary schools have formal school improvement plans which guide efforts to make them better. Obtain a copy of an improvement plan and see whether you can identify goal statements and improvement processes that clearly are related to making the school more democratic. Be prepared to specify characteristics or attributes of the statement(s) or process(es) that cause you to view them as democratic. If you cannot identify at least one goal and related improvement process that qualifies as democratic, describe how you would proceed—either as principal or as a staff member—to develop a goal intended to make the school more democratic along with the processes that would be used to meet the goal. Be prepared to present the results of your work.

4

WHAT DO YOU DO WHEN YOUR VALUES CLASH WITH THE SYSTEM'S?

Demands for higher levels of student performance affect activities in today's schools in fundamental ways (Berliner & Biddle, 1995). Parents and patrons rightly expect students to show convincing evidence of the benefits they derive from school. Many people assume students' scores on tests provide this evidence. This assumption provides clear incentives for schools to show continuous improvement in students' test scores.

Values driving such things as emphasis on test scores are increasingly shaped by the politics of special interests. The special interest that succeeds in focusing public attention on its concern also succeeds in reshaping the system's values via the input of focus groups upon whose inputs politicians rely (Spring, 1997). This, of course, severely limits the impartiality so morally essential to democratic discourse (Peters, 1980).

In a culture where news becomes stale within 24 hours, the loud persistent voice tends to wield the most influence (Postman, 1985). It is a serious concern, however, when values paraded as "what America needs" may in fact be highly visible representations of the agenda of a special interest group with an extraordinary ability to attract and maintain public attention.

Educators are seriously challenged to keep their personal values aligned with systemic values when the latter threaten to become more concerned with politics than with human need. Consider, for example, the inconsistency between the assertion espoused by *The National Education Goals Panel* (1994) that all children will start school ready to learn by the year 2000, and policies and practices enacted at the federal, state, and local levels that tolerate one child in four living in poverty.

The tensions between espoused and enacted values do little to ease the pressures on schools to initiate reforms. These pressures increase the complexity and challenge of school activities. Educators' lives are increasingly busy. Their responsibilities grow as classroom, school, district, state, and federal initiatives and mandates are implemented. Whether initiatives are undertaken in response to local, state, or federal insistence (McQuarrie, 1991), they are reflections of changes in values claimed to represent what is required for the system.

School leaders are held to high standards of performance as they address the burgeoning challenges of school improvement. These standards include multiple requirements for detailed, sophisticated knowledge and skill. They obligate contemporary school leaders to master many things. Leaders must effectively influence and guide initiatives for inclusion, curriculum expansion, accountability, assessment, and alternative methods of scheduling. They must deal with gang-related issues, address federally mandated goals, and take effective steps to ensure continuous improvement in measured student performance. They must assure anxious patrons that their schools are safe and drug free.

Competent leadership entails much more than just *knowing* about a plethora of complex tasks; it also includes expectations that the implementation of those tasks will be effectively managed and that attendant processes and products will be efficient and successful. The expectation for efficiency implies that all these things will be done in ways that appear effortless. These leader expectations require excellent judgment and interpersonal and decision-making skills. Moreover, appropriate attitudes or "dispositions" toward these and a host of additional "knowledges" and "performances" must be displayed (Interstate School Leaders Licensure Consortium, 1996).

As cultural diversity and complexity increase, it becomes more challenging to identify what may confidently be labeled a systemic value, let alone balance personal and system values. Leaders may begin to find themselves in conflict with the system. In the face of conflict with the system, individuals have theoretical access to four responses:

1. Fight the system and its values; force it to change.
2. Flee from the system and its values.
3. Achieve compromise between your values and the system's.
4. Surrender to the system's values.

Access to these alternatives is theoretical because practical considerations make it clear that some options are not open at all. It may be impossible to fight the system because influence or other necessary resources are lacking. It is important, too, to remember that the conclusion of an unsuccessful fight may be loss of position. It may be difficult to escape from the system because of dependency on income, fear of loss of reputation, negative sanctions, or fear of uncertainties accompanying flight. We also may find that we lack sufficient bargaining power to achieve an effective compromise. In the most limited circumstances, the only realistic alternative may be to resign ourselves to uncomplaining compliance with the system. In brief, we may think we—or our dependents—need the system or the job so desperately that surrender is the only option. When we find ourselves in these straits, we have reached what is variously called a crisis of conscience or a values dilemma.

This chapter provides suggestions for addressing crises of conscience. Suggestions and exercises are provided for assessing differences in values—the system's and ours, primarily—solving problems related to identified differences, and implementing solutions.

ASSESSING DIFFERENCES

Evaluating differences between personal values and the system's values presumes the *existence* of a difference. No *difference*, no *problem*. Our ability to evaluate the difference is attributable to status differentiation, a more or less formal phenomenon that significantly influences many aspects of human existence. Status differentiation is of central importance in any meaningful analysis of values. We examine it from two perspectives.

First, it is essential to note that status differentiation should be thought of as both bad and good—a paradoxical phenomenon. Status differentiation is an undesirable thing, for example, when it adversely and prejudicially affects equality of opportunity, especially equality of *educational* opportunity. From the second perspective, status differentiation is rightly taken to be desirable when it enables helpful distinctions to be made between alternative choices.

Do we not regularly distinguish between appropriate and inappropriate behavior? Educators do so routinely when they remind Jeffrey or Jill that their treatment of a classmate or situation was "inappropriate" or commend them for an action that was notably "appropriate." As long as Jeffrey and Jill view "the system" and its values as creators of legitimate moral obligation (Peters, 1980), compliance with what is held to be "appropriate behavior standards" is readily achieved.

Values are the criterial variables that enable individuals and entire cultures to appreciate and strive for quality and excellence (Bruner, Goodnow, & Austin, 1967; Gardner, 1961). Either solitary or team pursuit of excellence is paralyzed by inability to make qualitative distinctions. Failure to make appropriate distinctions allows inferior alternatives to replace better ones. In other words, when counterfeits either slip past careless judgment or go undetected by myopic observers, quality suffers (see Boorstin, 1961).

Because status differentiation can be used to achieve widely varied qualitative ends, it is clear that those who evaluate status differences must not only be able to detect qualitative differences among alternatives, they also must be able to evaluate the impact their choices make on the human condition. They must be effective moral and ethical agents (Sergiovanni, 1992).

This requirement obligates leaders to be effective custodians of such lower-order rules as are necessary to democratic existence and justifiable by reference to procedural principles—noninjury, keeping contracts, and respect for property, for example (Peters, 1980). The leader who is incapable of recognizing right human actions or of acting in their behalf should not work with children and youth. The reasons for this are self-evident and constitute one of the most powerful examples imaginable of the importance of making careful distinctions between alternatives.

As a further aid to evaluating differences between our values and the system's, we've turned, as we did in Chapter 3, to the fourth listed definition of *value* from *The American Heritage Dictionary, 2nd ed.* (1985): "A principle, standard, or quality considered worthwhile or desirable" (p. 1336).

The operative terms in the adopted definition are *principle* (a rule or standard, especially of good behavior); *standard* (an acknowledged measure of...value); *quality* (the essential nature of something; character); *worthwhile;* and *desirable.* As we reflect on how the benefits of the discussion might vary according to different meanings attached to worthwhile and desirable, we take *worthwhile* to mean "essential" and desirable to mean "needed." We will take the terms to be less optional than their ordinary meanings might suggest.

For purposes of the discussion, we will treat values as "those standards against which you regularly evaluate the quality of your own behavior." In other words, we treat values as synonymous with the words or expressions of belief by which we live. If values are to be things we can live by, however, they need to be effectively sorted and prioritized, knowing that if you don't stand for something, you'll fall for anything.

A POINT OF DEPARTURE

When explorers are in unfamiliar territory, they take careful note of prominent landmarks in order to keep their bearings. Because this is an exploration, we do a similar thing: We anchor the discussion in key assumptions, beliefs, and intentions. As you analyze the list, be aware that it is a compilation of values, and that you may want to identify others that you would have included. Also, some of the entries or similar ones appear elsewhere in the book.

**FIGURE 4.1. GROUNDING ASSUMPTIONS FOR A
COMPARISON OF PERSONAL AND SYSTEM VALUES**

---

1. It is possible to make useful distinctions between the qualities and worth of alternative values.

2. It is important to make thoughtful distinctions between alternative values.

3. Intrinsic motivation serves individuals, groups, and society better than extrinsic motivation.

4. Allowing ourselves to be unduly influenced or controlled by extrinsic motivators when assessing and adopting core values will "leave someone else in control."

5. Liberty is a key requirement in democratic forms of existence.

6. The liberty of individuals and groups to think and act is limited or qualified by the rights of others.

7. Some values are subjective and arbitrary to a certain degree.

These grounding assumptions imply important things. We have posited, for example, that intrinsic motivation is preferred to extrinsic motivation. Persuasive evidence supports this assertion (Kohn, 1993), but the practical implications of the assertion go far beyond the technical merits of formal evidence that supports it. In practical terms, core values will be impaired in fundamental ways so long as people hold them because something or someone "out there" expects that they should. In other words, as we assess and refine our core values, they shape the framework that defines our autonomy of thought, word, and action. It is a process that forms our identity—the essentials of our being—which should neither be surrendered nor taken lightly, particularly in a democracy.

Is this the same as saying that one should pay no attention to the thoughts, opinions, beliefs, or values of others as one shapes his or her own? Of course not; but as we say it, we realize that we are swimming against postmodernist currents, which hold that one person's perspective, point of view, interpreted meaning, or

value is as good as another's (see Leiser, 1973, on ethical relativism). Nevertheless, if we accept for the sake of argument that all
meanings are subjective and therefore unique and ungeneral-
izable, surely no one could object to our sharing *our* subjective
preferences, attempting to explain them, and inviting others to
adopt them as they feel it appropriate to do.

THE SPELUNKER'S STRING

Cave explorers unwind a string as they move into unfamiliar territory. This practice supplies a metaphor for a precaution
needed when embarking on a serious examination of core values. Examining core values can be hazardous to your health,
and explorers should therefore have ready access to dependable
emergency procedures.

Hazards arise when self-concepts are wounded by insensitive attack, and violence and injury result from physical confrontation over controversial topics. Preparation for discussion
of core values should include some potential "lifeline values"
that would provide help should the need arise.

Consider *leadership* as a possible core value. According to
Kouzes and Posner (1993), "above all else, people want leaders
who are credible" (p. 22). These authors believe credibility is associated with honesty, competence, and inspiration. Would we
be well advised to pick credibility, honesty, competence, or inspiration as our anchor—the core value we can count on in times
of confusion?

This question can be addressed through the use of a matrix.
Figure 4.2 is a 4x4 values matrix. The four columns are headed
by the values credibility, honesty, competence, and inspiration.
The four rows contain the same headings. The cells on the diagonal of the matrix are marked with an x, indicating where each
of the four values intersects with itself. The six cells above the diagonal contain a question mark, inviting you to compare credibility (being worthy of confidence) with honesty (integrity),
credibility with competence (being well qualified), with inspiration (emotional stimulation), and then to indicate which of the
two values being compared takes precedence. A straightforward way of indicating your six preferences is simply to draw

an arrow pointing in the direction of the value you prefer in each one of the six possible comparisons.

FIGURE 4.2. MATRIX FOR EVALUATING ALTERNATIVE VALUES

	Credibility	*Honesty*	*Competence*	*Inspiration*
Credibility	x	?	?	?
Honesty		x	?	?
Competence			x	?
Inspiration				x

How would your item-by-item comparisons look? If you compared credibility with honesty, which would be of greater worth? If you choose credibility over honesty, how would you respond to accusations that you are more concerned with your image than with telling the truth? What about the comparison of credibility with competence, credibility with inspiration, and so on through each of the six comparisons? (The six comparisons below the diagonal mirror those above and therefore are redundant for purposes of the comparisons being made.)

It is most certainly a generally useful thing if people are credible or believable, but does credibility serve purposes that are as basic as some of the other three? For example, what if someone is credible but incompetent—his or her advice has a believable ring, but following it would be surely mistaken and possibly costly as well?

We've suggested elsewhere that values that are objectively indistinguishable as to worth, influence, or impact are interchangeable for all practical purposes. We've also taken pains to point out that many values are objectively distinguishable. This point has important relevance for the present discussion. Do you agree that competence seems to play a more primary role or to fulfill a more important function than credibility?

What about the remaining two attributes, honesty and inspiration? We would quickly suggest that inspiration by itself would not serve productive purposes for extended periods of time. Pep squads can be helpful, but they tend to be at their best when there is something of substance to be peppy about. In the absence of competence, for example, inspiration is impotent. Similarly, if it is not tempered or informed by other values— keen perception, interpersonal sensitivity, and compassion, for example—the utility of honesty is limited.

As we tally our own results for the six comparisons, they turn out as follows: Credibility ranks only above inspiration, receiving one tally; honesty ranks above credibility and inspiration, receiving two tallies; competence ranks above credibility, honesty, and inspiration, receiving three tallies. In our conception of the ranking of these four values, therefore, competence is the primary value, honesty is the second most important, credibility is third (depending, as we see it, on the first two), and inspiration, because it was not ranked ahead of any other value, is a moderating value. That is not to say that inspiration is unimportant, but it does say that for our purposes, inspiration would be used in small doses to flavor and moderate the effects of the other three values.

It also is interesting to reflect on the utility of leadership itself as a core value. Leadership exists, to be sure. The exercise of leadership unquestionably makes a difference in the lives of people affected by it. Good leadership, moreover, may readily be recognized for the indispensable role it plays in situations where uncertainty and indecisiveness pose serious threats to necessary action. Having said all of this, however, it is imperative to understand the assumptions that undergird assertions about the indispensability of leadership.

First, an uncritical acceptance of the assertion that leadership is indispensable depends on the tacit assumption that followers are incapable of accomplishing independently whatever the leader is leading them to do. While it may very well be true that some of us will never acquire the knowledge and skill necessary to act autonomously in certain areas, we should nevertheless recognize the critical difference between knowing that we need assistance, guidance, or direction in *selected circumstances,* and believing we have a universal need for it.

A second, more serious assumption undergirding assertions about the indispensability of leadership is that it is fundamentally acceptable to assign followers to a status of perpetual dependency. Without the leader, according to this assumption, followers are incapable of acting. These two tacit assumptions—one related to assumed incapability and the other related to an assumed need for universal dependency—blatantly contradict one of the fundamental purposes of teaching: bringing learners, or *helping* them, to achieve a status where they think and act independently, competently, responsibly, and happily. We encourage readers to thoughtfully consider a question that is directly related to the issue at hand: *Is it better, as a value, to exercise leadership influence in ways that create perpetual dependency in the led, or is it better to lead in ways that liberate, or create responsible independence?*

It seems reasonably clear that *leadership,* as conventional wisdom sometimes conceives it, would not be desirable to adopt as a lifeline value to guide the *formulation of* core values. This assertion is directly related to and dependent on grounding the next three assumptions, having to do with intrinsic motivation, autonomy, and liberty. *If* intrinsic motivation, autonomy, and liberty are the compelling values we believe them to be, it seems reasonable to conclude that the elevated status traditionally associated with leadership should be lowered.

As you work through your analysis of the values that will anchor your comprehensive values framework you should note the possibility that leadership's feeder values of credibility, honesty, competence, and inspiration may not appeal to you as values that will anchor and influence your construction of a larger network.

A potential lifeline value we would offer for consideration: *Every person is entitled to have a comfortable and consistent sense of personal identity.* A second possibility: *Every person is entitled to derive meaning from his or her relationships with institutions.* The first lifeline value can be justified based on its consistency with good behavior—behavior that promotes health and happiness (Jefferson, 1776). It also can be justified based on the important role personal identity plays in the behavior of leaders. The second is justified on grounds that meaningful existence—experi-

encing things in our work, for example, that have "inner significance"—is as essential to a vital existence as nourishment,
shelter, health, and knowledge.

We also would offer for consideration as a lifeline value *the
freedom to refrain from talking about any topic that we choose.* If
among the first words heard by someone being arrested are
"you have the right to remain silent," how could one recommend less to a party with whom they hope to establish a beneficial understanding of something as important as core values?

Think for a moment about your sense of personal security or
self-confidence and your very best friend. Ask yourself how
personally secure or self-confident you really are, and then reflect on how you came to be very best friends with someone.
These questions are closely related. After all, is it not reasonable
to think of self-confidence as an important form of friendship
with oneself? And then, as you contemplate the question of how
people become best friends, does it seem to you as it does to us
that fast friendship emerges and takes hold chiefly as a consequence of time spent together and the discovery of deeply held
mutual interests, ideas, beliefs, values, and activities?

Let us offer a couple of conjectures about the notions of
self-regard and best friends. First, as is probably self-evident,
the better friend you are to yourself, the more comfortable, confident, natural, and easy you are around others, and the easier it
is to act with confidence in unfamiliar settings and situations.
Second, remembering that this is conjecture, we have an anec-
dotal sense that the more authentically self-confident one is, the
less necessary it is to demand compliance in thought, word, and
action from others.

In everyday terms, then, the person with a strong self-regard
should value strong personal identity in others, recognize the
essential nature of meaningful experience, and respect the reluctance of others to discuss certain things. In fact, insisting that an
individual discuss threatening or taboo topics not only belies
positive self-regard on the part of the one doing the demanding;
it also suggests a lack of respect for others, including respect for
the lifeline values of identity, meaningful experience, and self-
imposed silence. Before proceeding, take a moment to jot down
four or five values that you rely on for guidance during critical

junctures in your life. Do particular values tend to be constant for you—integrity, identity, competence, accurate information, expertise, love, courage, winning, or survival?

SETTING OFF TO SOLVE PROBLEMS RELATED TO VALUES DIFFERENCES

If you've identified values that will keep you connected with daylight and firm ground, start reeling out some string. The values-naming exercise we recommend may be completed solitarily, but a greater benefit might be realized if you carry out the activity as a group exercise. As few as 2 can participate productively, but the activity will be richer with 15 to 20 participants. Procedural suggestions are simple: if the number of participants is from two to six, three rounds of values naming are suggested. If your group is from 7 to 14, two rounds are recommended. Fifteen to 20 participants will find a single round of naming productive.

A round of values-naming entails having each participant specify a single value, remembering that participation is voluntary and electing to pass is acceptable. If one person names a particular value—optimism, for example—there is no prohibition of others naming it. As values are named, all participants should write them down. When one, two, or three rounds have been completed according to group size, individuals should review their lists and see whether any themes are evident—task orientation, learning, service to others, personal pleasure, or integrity, for example.

After all participants have reviewed their lists individually, have one member use large newsprint, an overhead transparency or chalkboard to list one participant's themes and the individual values assigned to that theme. For example, a *theme* might be labeled "relationships," and the values assigned to that theme might include positive attitude, family, people, respect, and learning with others. It's important to keep the notion of "criterial attribute" in mind as values are grouped thematically, remembering that criterial attributes are characteristics that allow things to be distinguished from other things, defined and grouped.

The value of this exercise lies in its capacity for contributing to a shared understanding of the meanings of various value concepts and of their potential or actual roles in improving the human condition. We are encouraging you to proceed based on yet another implicit, but nevertheless important value—that a "shared understanding" of what certain values "mean" is a desirable thing. This is not a recommendation to ignore what Peters (1980) calls "essential contestability," or the possibility that certain values will be seen as amorphous, debatable, subjective things with multiple meanings and, like beauty, will exist uniquely in the eye of the beholder. In other words, an "essentially contested value" is one which can be productively debated because of an absence of "one standard usage that can be taken as a model of correctness" (p. 67). That is not synonymous, however, with saying that a value is worthless simply because it is subject to multiple interpretations. The following passage from Bertocci (1980) illustrates the point: The included values are obviously "contestable," but certainly ones that promise to improve the human condition.

> In a more adequate discussion I would defend "a moral backbone," as it were, of *cardinal* virtues, inclusive at least of such traits as honesty, courage, kindness, gratitude, meekness, humility, fairness, justice, tolerance, and forgiveness (p. 101).

Lest anyone think we are recommending a totalitarian system of uniform values, we would encourage readers to think about the likelihood that diversity in values will be detected when two or more people are discussing them. Diversity is not just likely: In a democracy, resting as it necessarily must on a foundation of liberty, diversity is inevitable and to a significant degree desirable. It seems contradictory that values can or should serve as things that both unite and divide, but the careful reader will remember that paradoxical phenomena are like that. Further discussion of the paradoxical nature of values might, in fact, recommend *diversity* as a core value that is essential to human progress. That is, without diversity, none of what we are talking about would be possible, including tensions among competing ideas, differences of opinion, debates, syntheses, and change of any kind, including improvement.

Some concluding observations about the *personal* component of values exploration are in order. First, there probably is no prescribed number of "rounds" that will yield a result guaranteed to provide each participant with a trustworthy set of core values. It seems equally apparent, though, that the participants should be able to determine when the exercise has exhausted their capacities for gaining further benefits from it. This assumes, of course, that participants have brought a willing spirit and serious professional commitment to the experience. Next, we acknowledge the potentially contradictory nature of an exercise that is recommended to be carried out in a group setting, though intended to help *individuals* define core values. It should be obvious that individuals who are unsatisfied with their core values' status at the conclusion of the formal exercise should continue to work until they are content. Finally, we would point out (again) that the development of personal values is inevitably a work in progress and should not be thought of as something that will magically emerge at the conclusion of a single exercise. The exercise, in a word, is formative.

TURNING TO THE SYSTEM

Many commercially available frameworks are available to assist with values clarification. Personal planning systems may include a process for determining values as a foundation for managing time. These programs can facilitate and streamline the process of specifying one's values. Time invested in this way provides the yardstick against which to measure the importance and outcomes of decisions to be made. It will allow a leader to determine which battles to fight and which ones to ignore, tolerate, or abandon. In essence, personal values provide templates that are helpful in making decisions, especially difficult ones.

In serving as templates, values are useful when value-laden issues affect decision-making. In many situations, the act of evaluating a decision against a backdrop of relevant values tends to make the appropriate decision obvious. In a sense, the decision is already made, without the agonizing worry or procrastination in which so many are inclined to engage. The decision, as some like to say, becomes a "no-brainer."

At this point, there often is someone who desperately wants to remind everyone else that it's not always that simple or easy. They're right, of course. Consider what happens when principals find themselves making Faustian deals in attempts to serve conflicting ends—warning the powerful, abusive parent rather than making the report required by law, for example, in a misguided attempt to *both* protect the child *and* curry favor with the abuser. This is but one example of a class of challenging problems known as values dilemmas. These are situations in which one powerful value—survival, for example—is in threatening tension with some other powerful value such as serving justice. Those who learn, somehow, to serve justice at great personal risk are called courageous or said to have integrity or character. It is significantly more easy to describe the trait than it is to acquire it.

In the process of becoming courageous or acquiring character, the determination must be made first that there truly is a conflict with "the system." If you've succeeded at defining a trustworthy set of personal values, this process is much less difficult. Defining "the system" and its values provides a necessary framework or perspective to use in developing an understanding of the issue or conflict. The following questions provide an initial overview of the problem.

- ♦ Am I dealing with facts or perceptions as I define "the system"?

- ♦ Who—or what—am I considering to be "the system"?

- ♦ Is "the system" state mandates, board policy, district policy, building policy, or "something else"?

- ♦ Do I consider "the system" to be the culture of my school or district; that is, "the way we do things around here"?

- ♦ Is "the system" really a personality that changes when a new superintendent arrives?

- ♦ Is "the system" the global economy?

- Is it the federal government?
- Is it the state government?
- Is it the local district?
- Is it the PTA?
- Is it one of several booster clubs?
- Is it parents of gifted and talented students?
- Is it a clique of powerful teachers?
- Is it some combination of one or more of the above?
- Is it some organization, group, or individual other than the above?
- Is "the system" really an extraordinarily influential, low-profile citizen or small coalition of citizens?

As you ponder the possibilities, do not neglect to think about the influence of national and state organizations representing school boards, teachers, administrators, parents, or other organized interest groups focused on some special goal or feature of education—choice, charter schools, or home schooling, for example. You also might find it instructive to carry out an abbreviated sociometric analysis of patterned influences that affect practices in your school and district. In simplified form, this process entails asking a principal the name of the person or persons he or she has to check with before taking an important action. Next, check with that person and ask the same question, repeating the process until you (a) *begin to get repeated references* to a person, group, or organization; (b) *determine that lack of convergence or focus* on identifiable persons or groups suggests that values driving activities in your school are actually pretty diffuse; or (c) *find that the persons, groups, and values driving attempts to control and influence activities change* according to the content of specific issues. Grades, test scores, and standards, for example, may attract different advocates than proposed changes in human sexuality curricula or library holdings. Once you believe you have developed a defensible idea of who or what "the system" is in your situation and validated it, perhaps along lines suggested above, what's the next step?

We'd suggest that—within the context of your version of "the system"— you complete the following exercise: Start with several versions of "My school...." For these purposes assume that you're the principal, or imagine yourself to be. Once you think of "My school..." (for example, *shines, falters, excels, smells good, looks good,* or *suffers*), expand it a bit to "My school is (*a safe place, about kids, high tech, inviting, pretty poor, a sad place*), then "My school is a place where..." (all *participants do their best; some people fall through the cracks; everybody feels important; people love to come*), then "My school stands for..." (*nothing in particular; fairness; opportunity; excellence; rich experiences*), then, "At my school, we would never tolerate...." Once you've done this—identified the attributes or characteristics that evoke or imply important values for your school—try a variation of the exercise: This time, think about some feature of your school that could be changed for the better and say, "My school should...." Comparing your responses from the "My school is..." and "My school should..." statements will give you a set of discrepancies that can be used to tentatively identify areas of value structure that need to be changed. After you've done that, run through a similar protocol for "the system," completing these kinds of sentences:

"The system expects schools to...."

"The system expects schools to be...."

"The system insists that schools emphasize...."

"The system really doesn't care if schools...."

"The system believes schools aren't doing a good job unless...."

To assist with decision-making that will help you decide how well your values and your school's are aligned, how well your school's values and "the system's" are aligned, and whether anything needs to be done about any of those alignments, we provide a flowchart that illustrates critical situations and decision points of the process. The flowchart provides a concrete image to assist with the process of assessing circumstances, values, and decision making. It should encourage you to ask questions and consider options.

Figure 4.3. Values Choice Flowchart

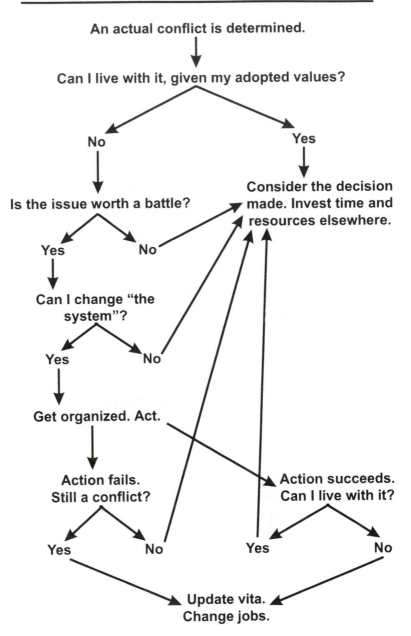

An actual conflict is determined.

Can I live with it, given my adopted values?

No

Yes

Is the issue worth a battle?

Consider the decision made. Invest time and resources elsewhere.

Yes

No

Can I change "the system"?

Yes

No

Get organized. Act.

Action fails. Still a conflict?

Action succeeds. Can I live with it?

Yes   No   Yes   No

Update vita. Change jobs.

True Conflict Is Determined

It is important to determine first whether conflicts actually exist rather than simply being perceived or anticipated. For example, states often prescribe rules or guidelines for schools and districts. School employees must be certain to adhere to the mandated regulations. It is important to not *presume* that a conflict or barrier exists.

State department employees from two states recently shared anecdotes describing requests from personnel in school districts. The requests were for *exemptions from state mandates that did not exist*. Barriers were perceived that weren't there. Miscommunication of this sort obviously represents wasteful use of time and energy and gives emphasis to the importance of *being certain conflict exists*. This is accomplished by talking with appropriate decision-makers and not relying on "the word around town." Once it is determined that a conflict exists, then decide whether you can live with it.

Can I Live with It, Given My Adopted Values?

Existence of an actual values conflict is the signal for a decision—unless you find uncertainty and indecisiveness particularly enjoyable. The relevant question is, "Can I live with it?" If you can live with it as it is, the decision is simple. Your energies can be invested in pursuits that are more important. This stage of the process is illustrated by the decision of a school's newly formed site council to assign parking spaces for staff. Time and energy would be devoted to that rather than addressing things the leader felt were more important. Although there is a conflict, she decides the issue can be lived with and chooses to invest time in more important issues, leaving parking to other, more interested parties. If the analysis leads to "no," the next choice to be made has to do with whether the issue is worth the battle.

Is the Issue Worth a Battle?

As leaders, we often hear that we must choose our battles. Again, having one's values clearly in focus helps make this determination. Answers to the battle question are conditioned in critical ways not only by your personal values and beliefs, but also by such things as (a) the extent to which a battle would place you at risk of severe personal loss; (b) the number of people who are dependent on you, the degree to which they share your values and beliefs, and the degree to which they can endure consequences of your losing the battle; (c) the risk that the battle would be lost; and (d) whether the value at stake is one where compromise— avoiding the battle—would have unbearable consequences. This discussion may remind you of personal experiences or stories you've heard from others. Have you ever agonized over a decision, or heard someone describe how difficult it is to do that? Have you been jarred from sleep by deepseated concerns about what will happen if you fail to do "the right thing"? Have you heard accounts of leaders who took a path of lesser resistance on a really difficult decision, only to discover too late that "losing" in an attempt to do the right thing could not possibly have cost as much?

Decisions of this sort are the kinds that prompt Sergiovanni to write of moral leadership (1992), covenants, and leadership by outrage (1995). They are not to be taken lightly, and they probably comprise a category of concern that observers would do well to treat with empathy for those who are experiencing them. The lesson—or *moral* —is important enough to emphasize: In our experience, leaders of extraordinarily good reputation tend to share a reluctance to be visibly and vocally critical of perceived shortcomings in others, especially those who may indicate tentative or ambiguous moral courage. In short, if they can say nothing *good*, they remain silent.

This tendency—to remain silent if you cannot speak well of another—is an exemplar of the kind of behavior that we have come to associate with extraordinarily effective leadership. It is behavior that tends, generally, to be associated with trustworthy circumspection: If you cannot speak well of another, remain silent. We are probably not sufficiently wise to describe the inestimably worthwhile value that undergirds this kind of behavior. We can only reflect on the commendable value of reputations made from this sort of behavior. We would encourage you to think deeply about the implications of behaving in ways that deserve this kind of tribute. What is it, really, that makes those who speak ill of no one so remarkably memorable? What is the value that prompts reticence? It seems to be a value worth contemplation.

SUMMARY

In this chapter, we considered alternatives that can be pursued when we find ourselves at odds with "the system." We addressed the four primary responses available to one whose values fail to coincide with values that are apparent in prevailing patterns of influence: fight, flight, compromise, and surrender. We also addressed the need to anchor ourselves in dependable territory when embarking on explorations of values that may be so unfamiliar as to be threatening. Values, after all, are things that have wide-ranging powers. They can divide almost as easily as they unite. Because principals work in systems which have values that may be at odds with the values that principals bring to them, it is important that practitioners understand the prevailing values of whatever "system" they find themselves in.

Once that fundamental understanding is achieved, it is equally important to understand what can be done when your values are incompatible with those that prevail in the system of which you're a part.

ACTION FOLLOW-UP

♦ It certainly is interesting and perhaps even contradictory that Americans, as a culture, tend to think *their* school is "just fine, thank you," but other schools are inadequate. Find out how *your* school stands with regard to this assertion. Do *your* staff, students, and patrons think your school is "just fine," or do they find significant fault with it?

♦ Depending on what you learned in the first follow-up item above, do one of the following: (a) If your school is viewed positively, see how your respondents perceive other schools. Do they tend to attribute positive achievements to them as well, or do responses tend to be similar to the "ours is okay, others are not" pattern? (b) If your school is described as okay and others are criticized, find out the underlying causes—values—that support the response. If you find evidence of systemic values at work—values influenced by politicians' comments, state department reports on achievement, national reports, or United States Department of Education studies—specify them in sufficient detail to enable you to draw implications, both for your school and for the "system of schools" nationwide. Describe the implications.

♦ As an educator whose professional emphasis is leadership, you might agree that your responsibilities transcend interests that apply only to your school. If you do agree, think about what you, as a single, sometimes solitary leader can and should do to change public perceptions of "the system" so that public views of all schools will improve and, at the same time, the gulf that exists between "my good school," "the school system," and "the system at large" will be reduced.

♦ With one or more partners discuss and describe differences between what "the system" will require of schools in the future and then reflect on and describe what those expectations will imply for your school and for schools at large. Would you predict that schooling in general and public schools in particular would tend more to be challenged or to thrive given what your predictions about "the system" suggest?

5

CONSISTENCY AND NONCONTRADICTION

This chapter addresses attributes of behavior that serve functions analogous to those served by the Rosetta Stone. You may recall that the Rosetta Stone provided the key required to decipher hieroglyphics, which had been indecipherable prior to the famous stone's discovery. The three separate sets of symbols on the stone permitted interpreters to glean meaning from the unknown through the dependable bridge provided by the known—in this case, Greek.

Consistency and noncontradiction are analogous in that they provide links and touchstones in behavior that allow others to see how intentions conveyed in one of our acts are logically and convincingly related to intentions we want to convey in others. In other words, consistency and noncontradiction among assertions and actions convey purposeful, unconfusing meaning and provide crucial defining evidence of a principal's system of values and beliefs.

We discuss here what practitioners intuitively have come to call "walking the talk." To "walk the talk" is to hold and espouse exemplary goals, then act in ways that effectively support and reinforce the espousals. To behave in this way, consideration must be given to "the talk" and its origins. This chapter proceeds from the introduction to a reconsideration of pragmatic arguments for rejecting moral relativism. We move then to discussion of what will be referred to as manifestations, or evidence of values and beliefs that are effectively integrated. Among these manifestations are the messages we send and the "voices" we use in sending them. We consider how consistency is supported and strengthened by consciously searching for incongruence and dissonance among various aspects of behavior, and by creating approaches that maximize the goodness of fit among thoughts, words, and actions.

INTRODUCTION

A cynical joke drives home the imperative importance of principals being consistent.

Question: *How can you tell if your principal's lying?*

Answer: *If the principal's lips are moving, he's lying.*

You may argue that the joke is misapplied if our intent really is to emphasize the importance of consistency. "Actually," you may think, "principals who lie every time they talk are behaving *very* consistently!" True enough. The point should not be overlooked, though, that the principal who consistently lies is clearly acting inconsistently with the expectation that he will be truthful. Hence, the implicit lesson of the joke is don't be inconsistent in this way unless you want to be held in contempt or destroy your credibility and with it, your leadership (Kouzes & Posner, 1993).

The idea that consistency is desirable is both a values position and an empirical fact. It is a values position inasmuch as it holds that consistent behavior is preferred to erratic behavior. Its empirical justification is found in the *regularly patterned criticisms* of principals who are disruptively and counterproductively *in*consistent:

> You could never tell from one day to the next how Mr. Blank would react—peaches and cream one minute, vinegar the next.

> Oh, sure! You could always count on old Farnsworth! He was 100 percent unpredictable!

> With Ms. von Baden you just couldn't ever be sure. One day she would throw the book at a kid for inappropriate behavior. The next, she'd chew you out for your poor handling of exactly the same thing.

> I guess teachers are supposed to be able to handle unfair treatment. After all, we're adults. We're expected

to understand that life's not always fair. But the poor kids! They always groused behind Mrs. Bleep's back about how she favored her friends' kids when they got into trouble. They complained even more bitterly about what a hypocrite she was—always harping about justice being one of life's most important virtues.

As you reflect on these examples, you might recall others from your own experience, giving special effort to remembering the critical, wry, cynical tone of voice colleagues use in describing inconsistent principal behavior. You also will want to recall the slump-shouldered resignation and hopelessness in nonverbal behaviors that accompany these descriptions. Both tone and nonverbal aspects indicate frustration, disappointment, and lack of respect.

In its most fully developed form, this sort of criticism may burst out of its banks in an angry faculty forum. Imagine how you would feel if a mature, respected faculty member stood in the middle of a heated discussion of your performance and said: "You just don't get it. The fact is, the vast majority of people here hold you in contempt. They may not say it to your face, but I will, and it's the truth!" You may find such behavior lacking in professionalism, but that should not divert you from thinking about the competent, consistent kinds of behavior required to prevent the criticism.

As you think about consistency, remember that it is not simply an adjunct, corollary, or naive byproduct of coherent values and beliefs. In its most persuasive and effective forms, *consistent, noncontradictory behavior depends on and is caused by thoughtfully conceived and coherently organized values and beliefs*. This is really self-evident. It also should be carefully noted that *consistency is both a standard for judging the goodness or desirability of a particular set of well-integrated beliefs and values* and a defining attribute of coherency in values and beliefs.

Talk of *dependency, cause, standards, and attributes* may be confusing, so before going too much further we need to explicitly acknowledge some challenges associated with the consideration of consistency and noncontradiction. You may wonder how it is possible to claim that your values and beliefs are coherent when at times they clearly are not—being consistent, but flexible, for instance, as Abraham Lincoln is said to have been (Phillips, 1992). Frustration and confusion might be relieved by recalling that behavior can be paradoxical—one thing *and* another—consistent *and* flexible. It probably becomes apparent that the kinds of sorting, sifting, selecting, and application entailed in harmonizing values and beliefs is a dauntingly complex and challenging activity—one not readily given to a straightforward, sequential, simplistic, unqualified approach.

We have seen time and again that leaders whose behaviors are anchored in carefully grounded and effectively integrated values and beliefs do not behave in self-contradictory ways as often as those whose values and beliefs are less coherently ordered. Even paradoxical leader behaviors tend to make sense to others because they are arguably complementary.

To examine this assertion in more detail, we offer the following propositions: We propose that frameworks of values and beliefs serve better where *tolerance* is given priority over *intolerance* and *acceptance* is held to be superior to *tolerance*. It follows from this line of thinking that *solidarity* with others is superior to *acceptance*.

Having said this, we must reemphasize not only the possibility, but also the desirability of behaving paradoxically—to be *intolerant* of child abuse, for example, while simultaneously arguing that tolerance is a generally good behavior. Similarly, we would suggest that while solidarity with others is generally superior to acceptance and tolerance, it still is not a contradiction to *avoid* establishing solidarity with individuals and groups who espouse values, beliefs, and practices known to be harmful to the effective education and overall nurturing of children, youth, and adults.

Solidarity of compelling purpose in a school allows learners to be influenced more effectively and positively than those in more matter-of-fact, routine environments. Consider a proposal to move a school toward a promising innovation. Think of the difference in meaning between teachers who say: "I could accept that," and others who say: "I would *love* that!" If you are the principal, which response is more encouraging? Would the passive agreement connoted by "I could accept" contribute as optimistically to a successful outcome as "I would *love...*?" Grudging acquiescence is not on a par with enthusiastic support as a value, and it certainly does not contribute as richly to the creation and maintenance of *esprit* and otherwise positive climate.

Does this mean that principals should *require* everyone to be enthusiastic? In our view, it clearly would not, inasmuch as an expectation of mandatory enthusiasm contradicts avowals of belief in freedom of expression, participation, and empowerment. It also lowers the probability that better decisions will be made when colleagues are free to point out flaws and suggest improvements. So, while we see solidarity of support for compelling causes as a good thing to value in schools, we also see it as good to avoid insisting that everyone *must* achieve solidarity, because doing so reflects a lack of respect for individual autonomy and freedom of choice.

Having said this, we would hasten to acknowledge that some principals give primary emphasis to their personal authority and power. In doing this, they fail to address colleagues' basic needs for recognition, consideration, and respect. This critical omission often leads to feelings of marginalization and disenfranchisement on colleagues' parts. Because the values of authentic inclusion and involvement are neglected, they will be displaced, in due time, by isolation and indifference.

Aspiring and practicing principals should not take this to mean that we discourage the use of persuasion as they attempt to influence others to support worthy causes. Differences in values, after all, create the necessary tensions that cause us to question and reshape our beliefs and values.

It can be both a complicating and stimulating fact that others do not share this viewpoint. There are those who will happily and confidently tell you what to value, what to believe, and how to behave in fairly specific, precise, and limited ways. Because that approach runs counter to foundational principles of liberty and freedom, we believe the aforementioned emphasis on *persuading* others to adopt certain values and beliefs is imperatively important—persuading that values and beliefs *do* make critical differences in the human condition—but that they must, if they are to have lasting effects, be thoughtfully formulated and *voluntarily* put into practice (see Strike, Haller, & Soltis, 1998).

Values and beliefs are abstractions and therefore tend to not lend themselves to direct observation and the kind of empirical study that can be applied, say, to physics or chemistry. It is not possible, for example, to tell an aspiring principal how to develop consistent values and beliefs in ways that are comparable to telling a chemistry student how to make sulfuric acid. In fact, given their abstract, complex, highly subjective nature, values and beliefs are subjects that have a real potential to be so opaque, controversial, and frustrating that students will be discouraged from successfully confronting them. That, we believe, would be unfortunate and regrettable.

Any full discussion of consistency and noncontradiction in values and beliefs must recognize that tyrants whose values were nothing if not single-mindedly integrated have slaughtered millions of human beings. What, then, are we attempting to encourage in aspiring and practicing principals? Essentially, we espouse that some of the fundamental content of values and beliefs and their patterns of integration are preferred because their effects on the human condition are more beneficial than the effects of other approaches that might be adopted. It is better to love, for example, than to hate; better to nurture than to impoverish; better to share than to hoard; better to teach effectively than to confuse.

Are these assertions universally true as expressions of values and beliefs? Is love *always* to be preferred to hate, or would it be more accurate and thoughtful to say that love is *usually* or *sometimes* better than hate—but not always? A moment's reflection may reveal occasions when it is appropriate or even desirable to hate some particular thing: child abuse, for example, or teaching that is deliberately indifferent. Further thought may similarly suggest that the human condition would be better served if totalitarian regimes were deliberately impoverished by humanitarian movements, or that hoarding certain materials in service to some idealistic end would be justified on occasion.

Just as tyrants slaughter innocents, instances are evident throughout recorded history in which fundamental values differences in ideology, philosophy, and religion have either fueled or been used as pretexts for subjugation and control. In the latter days of the 20th century, there is a continuing readiness on the part of some individuals and groups either to impose certain values, beliefs, and practices on acquiescent targets, or to devise and pursue means by which uncooperative peoples either may be controlled or marginalized. Instances of this sort range from insistence by certain religionists that public schools either be "reformed" or destroyed (Berliner, 1997) to those in which radicals and international terrorists see fit to murder large numbers of people in the service of some particular conviction or aim.

Are things of this sort avoidable, or are they inevitable? Should individuals and groups compromise values and beliefs to the point of sacrifice of conscience and the enduring of personal humiliation, or should they resist—even to the point of martyrdom? Should any person or group have the unilateral right to impose their will on other persons or groups, or should certain "rights" be universally recognized? Should power be the ultimate arbiter of behavior? Should money? Should real, or threatened, abuse?

These are the kinds of thorny, sticky, and potentially paralyzing issues out of which a system of values and beliefs must be forged. As you read these words you may find them sobering, but we hope you will not neglect to remember that they still describe the kinds of alternative values issues and positions which at the very least allow—and often *cause*—cultures to advance and decline. Are people and situations capable of improvement or not? Do our individual and interactive experiences occur according to predestined pattern, or do we enjoy at least some discretionary latitude within which our values, beliefs, and the related decisions and choices play influential parts? What does your experience suggest with regard to these questions? What, if anything, does it encourage you to make of yourself as a thoughtful, effective servant-leader? What kinds and quantities of risk, effort, commitment, and investment are justified by the potential benefits?

Perhaps the difficulty associated with developing a coherent framework of values and beliefs can be both illustrated and leavened through humor, and perhaps through the lens of humor you may be persuaded that values and beliefs are worth your time and struggle. Two stories will serve.

In the first, one person asks another: "Would you like to be rich and not have to work?" The second, visibly excited, replies that he would—very much! "Well," said the interrogator, "first, get a lot of money!"

In the second story, an ecstatic student tells a professor that she has just been appointed to her first middle-school principal-ship. After appropriate congratulatory comments, the professor asks the student if she would like some indispensable advice. The student, avidly interested, said that she would—very much! "Well," intones the Professor, "don't overlook anything that's really important!"

An important observation about the stories is that in each instance, the recipient of the "advice" points out that it is not only cruel, but worthless, to which the advisor replies: "Well, I've just given you the theory. It's up to you to work out the details."

There's a risk we'll do something similar in this consideration of consistency. We may tend to ask: "Would you like some advice that will really help you become an effective leader?" to which you reply, "O, golly, yes!" We then say, "Well, just be sure that your values and beliefs are consistently and coherently organized around laudable, noble causes, and make sure that your behavior reflects your values and beliefs."

This advice, of course, requires that behavior should be substantially consistent with what principles of justice signify as "good." This, as you have probably already discerned, is a fairly big trick. The "trick," in fact, is to develop and organize your values, beliefs, and behaviors in ways that make their commitment to justice transparent. One way of doing this was suggested by John Rawls (1971). Rawls posited that a just society would be likely to result from a process in which any given person would be allowed to design the social system, but only under terms of a strict condition. That strict condition says the designer may specify whatever roles are desired, and then assign any responsibilities, authority, and status to those roles that he or she wishes. The "catch," though, is that the designer may have no *a priori* knowledge of, or voice in assigning, whatever role the designer is to play in the resultant society. Rawls's theory, of course, is that any one of us who had such a task would be strongly motivated to design a just system. It is very much like the parent who strives to teach her children about fairness by having one child divide an orange and then giving the second child first chance to pick a piece.

It may help to note that the stories about "advice" use farce to make their jokes. The stories farcically suggest that there are easy solutions to difficult problems. We hope they emphasize a very important point: There is no simplistic answer to the question, "What should *I* value and believe?" The *thoughtful* acquisition of *any* consistently and helpfully integrated system of values and beliefs is the work of a lifetime. The acquisition of a coherent, influential, and socially beneficial system of values and beliefs is not only the work of a lifetime, but grindingly difficult as well. It requires conscious effort, perseverance, discerning judgment, high tolerance for ambiguity and confusion, and an unwavering dedication to noble and virtuous causes.

Those causes should be ones you are able to conceive and defend with a clear conscience and glad heart. This may be confusing because it seems to suggest that values are relative after all. Three critical reminders will relieve any potential confusion: (a) The belief that all values are relative is an absurdity, inasmuch as it negates the possibility of distinguishing among values and therefore denies the possibility of choosing among values. (b) While attributes of some values allow those values to be absolutely preferred to others (poison or palliative), others have attributes that make the value paradoxical (love is *both* a blessing *and* a curse). (c) If individual freedom is to be protected, then the imposition of systems of values on reluctant or unsuspecting recipients negates individual freedom and therefore underlines the importance, for *free* peoples, of their retaining the free right to choose those values and beliefs that they believe will best preserve their own and others' freedoms.

Our hope is that you will have the patience and perseverance to develop values and beliefs that will enable you to develop what Sergiovanni (1995) calls covenantal relationships with others, and that those relationships will enable you to serve your students in heroic ways. When we establish covenants with others, we enter into agreements that are soberly assumed —agreements that others recognize for their sacred, faithful, "I will never let you down" qualities. Our ability to establish covenantal kinds of relationships with others, and—perhaps as importantly—our *reputation* for this sort of behavior, tends to be recognized for its solid grounding in values such as loyalty, among others. As you reflect on your present tendencies and future aspirations, you might find it helpful to think about where you would like colleagues to place you on the following continuum.

FIGURE 5.1. VALUES SHAPE RELATIONSHIPS

How will others view you?

More like this?	*or*	*More like this?*
Loyal supporter		Fair-weather friend
Constant		Erratic
Dependable		Undependable
Predictable		Unpredictable
Grounded		Confused
Courageous		Timid
Principled		Unprincipled
Ethical		Unethical

When values and beliefs are thoughtfully conceived and applied, their observable consequences can become primary materials in the creation of a healthy, cohesive, creative school culture. The principal who is a coherent, exemplary model for students, staff, and patrons can become a memorably influential figure. Principals like this serve as incubators for the traditions and legends found in culturally rich school environments. Recall the complimentary descriptions of memorable leaders: "I would follow her anywhere." "I would trust him with my life." "You could always depend on her." "I never had a moment's doubt about where I stood with him."

What would you like colleagues to say about you?

PRAGMATIC ARGUMENTS
AGAINST RELATIVISM

A former student argued most soberly, seriously, and sincerely that *all* values, as long as they are "out there"—not directly applied to particular circumstances—are relative. In making that assertion, he wanted to be understood to say that all values are equal until they are applied to a specific situation.

You may agree that "out there values" are relative—applicable and meaningful to (and binding only on) those who hold them. You also may note, however, that affirmation of an assertion of this sort is irrelevant to the pragmatic realities of human interaction and quality of life. It is the practical equivalent of saying: "My thoughts, interpretations, and actions are irrelevant to anyone but me." "What you don't know, won't hurt you," or "We'll never know what Josh might have become if only he'd lived longer." Statements of this sort may be abundantly and self-evidently true in a technical sense, but they are pointless, inasmuch as their truth is incapable of making a positive difference in anything we might experience in the future, either individually or in relationships with others.

But all values are not relative, as we have already argued. While *some* values *are* relative, all values clearly are not relative because it is patently obvious, for example, that the values represented by aspirin and arsenic, respectively, are neither "out there" nor comparable. Reasonable people would not argue for a moment that a lacing of drain cleaner in baby's morning pablum will have effects no different from a comparable amount of sugar. Similarly, informed persons would not argue that feet, bicycles, and automobiles are equivalent transportation values, or that Harvard and Waybelow Normal U. are equivalent educational values. Recall that *choice* would be unnecessary *and* impossible if all values were equal; this assertion leads to the inescapable conclusion that without choice, the entire realm of decision making would neither be necessary nor possible.

Interestingly, if truth is "relative"—only ethically meaningful to the person or group that holds it (*The American Heritage Dictionary, 2nd ed.*, p. 1043), then it literally would not or could not make any difference what individuals and groups hold to be true; that is, what they believe or value. If some particular truth—*veritas*—has ethical meaning only for the person or group that holds it, then the concepts of truth and agreement or consensus lose their meaning. If all values and beliefs were relative, this narrative would be pointless, and an entire book on the role of values and beliefs in administrative performance would be even more pointless. Some may argue that the effort *is* pointless. But that assertion really emphasizes the argument against relativism rather than refuting it, because it serves again to underline the existence of values differences and emphasize their importance.

The point is emphasized by another interjection of humor. A pragmatist and a postmodernist were conversing. The postmodernist asserted with imperious confidence that narratives have no inherent meaning. "They only mean what various readers *feel* they mean, not what authors may have intended." The pragmatist countered wryly: "Surely, my friend, you can't expect me to believe that you *mean* what you just *said*." Particular emphasis should be given to the postmodern tendency to assert that nothing is inherently or explicitly meaningful, and to the explicit contradiction postmoderns set up when they declare— sometimes with smug confidence: "Nothing is meaningful." The assertion, of course, contradicts itself. This sort of thing should be sedulously avoided if we aspire to consistency among our thoughts, words, and actions.

MANIFESTATIONS OF CONSISTENCY AND NONCONTRADICTION

As you think about your own evolving system of values and beliefs, it may be helpful to remember that consistency and noncontradiction are not well served by attempts to hold patently incompatible beliefs in mental storage simultaneously, for instance, "all people are good; no person is trustworthy" or "effort counts; ability is everything." Remember that the statement "all values are relative" is self-contradictory and inconsistent.

Do you wonder how that can be so? If you think about it for a moment, you may recognize that "all values are relative" is an absolute. It asserts that *all* values, without exception, are relative. Formal logic, though, tells us that if *all* values are truly relative, we may not say it or even believe it, because to do so takes an absolute position and therefore contradicts the assertion.

The point might be made in this way: Most people who have been treated unfairly by teachers who valued control more than satisfying a child's curiosity would agree that values and beliefs are important features of behavior. Some might suggest that in many cases—not all, of course—differing degrees of merit or desirability can be attached to different values. Some would even go so far as to suggest that a collection of arguably meritorious values and beliefs becomes even more usefully valuable when it is coherently and noncontradictorily integrated.

Is this the same as saying that no two alternatives are comparable? Of course not! Most of us have some awareness of the idea that alternate paths can lead to the same goal (the concept of equifinality). Many of us remember ways of getting from A to B which were comparable in most of their critical aspects. And who would argue that the value of a vacation either in New York or San Francisco might not be essentially comparable for some people?

Comparability of *some* values is not really the important point. What *is* essential to recognize and remember is this: Many important values and beliefs differ pretty significantly, and this fact not only makes decision making possible, it also underscores the critical role played by our ability to evaluate and then act on those differences.

As we talk about saying what we mean and then acting consistently with our talk it occurs to us to point out some of the important influences exerted by differences in values are reflected in equally important differences in behavior. Think, for example, about the difference in values represented by the following statements: (a) I will not lie if I can help it, and (b) I will always tell the truth unless doing so will result in harm. Both statements reflect a nominal commitment to telling the truth, but there is a difference in the valence of the two statements. In the first instance, the emphasis is on avoiding a socially inappropriate behavior. In the second, active engagement of a socially desirable behavior is advocated.

Let us speak more directly about the *manifestations*—outward, observable evidence—of values and beliefs that are effectively integrated and harmonized. For illustrative purposes, our total system of values and beliefs can be conceptualized as a continuum. At one end are values and beliefs that are clearly and unambiguously consistent. As the continuum is examined from end to end, one may think of elements of value and belief toward the center as being less consistent, but not overtly and unarguably contradictory. These may be accurately and helpfully referred to as *complementary*. At the other end are those values and beliefs that are clearly contradictory. The principal who lives at this end of the continuum will likely have his or her manifestations of values and beliefs described with words such as *inconsistent, arbitrary*, and *unfair*.

FIGURE 5.2. A VALUES-BELIEFS CONTINUUM

Values and beliefs are:

Consistent	Complementary	Contradictory
(Illustrative descriptors associated with each)		
Trustworthy	Understandable	Undependable
Fair	Judicious	Arbitrary
Wise	Thoughtful	Reactionary
Solid	Forgivable	Fractious

As you think about your own efforts to make your values and beliefs more internally consistent, it may be helpful to mentally list labels for concepts that describe what you are after. Examples of labels—with their opposites— that we have found helpful in this endeavor include: harmony (discord); consonance (dissonance); reconciliation (conflict); integrity (flaws);

comfort (disturbance); pleasure (pain); wise (foolish); integrated (segregated); tranquil (turbulent); seamless (patchwork); invitational (repulsive).

As you consider these pairs (and add others of your own), begin to think deliberately, systematically, and productively about what you value and believe. Work, as it were, from your core out, or from the foundation up. Can you identify one or more values that you hold central to your identity and treat as primary navigational aids to direct the course of your existence? Would education, perhaps, be one? Would loyalty? Integrity? Self-reliance? Unflagging effort to improve? Are one or more of your core values related to things or issues that you take to be unshakably nonnegotiable? As you sort, sift, and prioritize them, do certain values have attributes and hold meaning that convince you of their central, foundational role in your life and professional career? Have you already, for instance, begun thinking along lines such as: "I value loyalty as a primary barometer, compass, and guidepost; therefore, I will always act in ways that reinforce colleagues' confidence in my constant, fair support"? Note that the value *loyalty* is followed by the statement of belief: "Therefore, I will always...."

As we think further about foundation and evidence, core and manifestation, it is instructive to recall aphorisms that powerfully illustrate the importance of consistency and noncontradiction:

> What you do speaks so powerfully that I cannot hear what you say.

> Do as I say, not as I do.

What do these negative, perhaps ill-chosen, examples convey as to intent or meaning? In the first example, from the perspective of an observer, the clear message is that we cannot fairly expect others to behave in exemplary ways if our personal model or example is inappropriate. In the second case, this time from the "leader," the proverb clearly signifies, this time through irony, that an authority figure has no right to expect bad examples to beget good behavior.

FINDING YOUR VOICE

Things usually are found as a consequence of one of two conditions. First, we may have once "had" something, but misplaced it. Hence, we see the first condition under which we need to find the thing. It is lost. Second, we may *find*—as in acquire, cultivate, or develop—a skill, talent, or behavior that we have not previously had and therefore not used. We learn to walk, talk, swim, ride bikes, sing, dance, whistle, drive, think, and give talks or speeches. Many of these "found things" will be recognized as ways of behaving that really do not require much encouragement for us to seek them more or less avidly. Many of them, moreover, are ways of behaving that often are learned without the assistance of formal teachers and teaching (Pinker, 1997). For many of us, finding our voice tends to be less natural than walking, talking, or following the course we have claimed is important.

Voice tends to be *found* in the second sense discussed earlier. We find it by a process of discovery, experimentation, practice, and reshaping. Its nature varies as dramatically as the numbers of individuals using it and the nature of environments in which it is raised. Principals who have particularly effective voices learn to speak in passionately moving and persuasive ways. Their messages often address inspiring themes. A new principal, for instance, wins the affection and support of her staff by talking with authority and conviction about three things: One, let your students know that what you do in school is important. Two, let them know that you'll always do your best. Three, let them know that you'll never give up on them.

How do *you* find *your* voice? You will most probably find it through an arduous process of trial and error unless you are one of those rare individuals who has a "gift" or intuitive feel for speaking.

However you acquire it, an *influential* voice depends first on sensitively accurate knowledge of the nature of the intended audience. If you do not "know" your intended recipients, your messages will have effects which are influenced more by chance than by deliberate, informed design. When the intended audience is understood, an influential voice relies on resonant content for its success. By resonant, we refer metaphorically to the ability of some messages to set up sympathetic vibrations in hearers to attract, engage, and then galvanize them to action.

The ability to move others to action through the exercise of voice, in our view, also should be moderated by vigilant sensitivity to the fact that using a persuasive voice to recommend particular ends and means must be undertaken in ways that are irreproachably moral and ethical. Moral and ethical content, of course, is the direct descendant of values and beliefs. One of the most sobering causes for reflection in this observation is wrapped in the realization that our exertions of influence all carry the potential to *degrade*, *maintain*, or *improve* their intended targets.

The resigned assertion of an exhausted principal, claiming that "what I think, say, and do doesn't make any difference" may accurately be called an absurd tragedy. The assertion is absurd because it is obviously untrue. It is tragic because of the nature of its consequences, whether they are intended or not. Principals, among other educators, have significant, weighty responsibilities for the welfare of their students, communities, and colleagues. A failure to recognize that and a failure to recognize what one means in saying, "I don't make any difference" is not only to fail, but to fail miserably.

MESSAGE

If you are to use your voice clearly, consistently, and influentially in support of morally defensible aims, *message* must be addressed. More specifically, essential elements of effective messages need to be thoughtfully considered.

The important elements of principals' messages include: *audience:* those you intend to influence by means of your message; *content*: what you intend to convey; *clarity:* the transparent, unambiguous meaning of your intended communication—what it brings to mind; *fluency:* the unconfused, uninterrupted *flow* of your intended message; *fidelity:* the faithfulness of themes, phrases, clauses, modifiers, parenthetic comments, gestures, emphases, and so forth, to your central or primary purposes for communicating; *static*: the tendency, however unwitting or unintentional, to wander from your theme or to introduce distracting or confusing verbal or nonverbal content.

We also think it may be helpful to mention *tenor,* or general character and tendency, as in: "The *tenor* of Mr. Bland's comments was...." In place of the ellipses, we might insert terms such as informative, helpful, calm, cordial, confrontational, invitational, inspiring, irritable, and so forth. Vocal inflection, nuance, gesture, personal comfort, and confidence all convey *meaning* to your audience, and these meanings will be conveyed whether you intend them or not.

Given this irrevocable probability, you may agree that it will be better for all concerned if you begin with a clear understanding of what you intend to communicate and then speak and act in ways that convey your intentions in clear, unconfusing ways. It also may be helpful to think of another term—*affordance*—which is described by Edward S. Reed (1996) as the *potential* of a particular value to yield benefits. In other words, certain values *afford* or *offer* certain opportunities.

In thinking about how principals develop and use their voices in behalf of desirable ends, tapestry may provide a useful metaphor. If you think of the sum of your values, beliefs, education, responsibilities, aptitudes, and skills as the threads and yourself as the artist, you can then begin to envision weaving those various strands into a harmonious, balanced, pleasing, compelling, durable, and dynamic work.

Your metaphor may be different. Rather than threads, you may prefer to think of elements. Instead of tapestry, you may choose to think of an elegantly played game, well-written novel, or beautifully composed musical work. In any one of these instances it is crucial to remember and appreciate the materials with which you work and, equally important, your role as the artisan who continuously arranges and rearranges those materials successfully and effectively. It also is important to remember that the work, however conceived, is dynamic—an evolving work in progress.

As we think along these lines, it is appropriate to return to a more direct consideration of consistency and noncontradiction: saying what you mean, meaning what you say, and acting in ways that consistently support both. We are complex mixtures of ambition, competence, and conscience. When the three are nicely balanced, life tends to go well. When they're not, those who have to spend time around us tend to become frustrated and confused because our reach (ambition) sometimes exceeds our grasp (competence), and our conscience, or lack of it, more properly, is not sufficient to temper, compensate for, or brake either our ambition or our ignorance.

Mihaly Csikszentmihalyi (1997) points out that Freud's ego, id, and superego are analogous to ambition, competence, and conscience. This suggests how values and beliefs interact with and fuel behavior. Ambition, for instance, is an essential ingredient in achievement of any kind. Ambition is necessary to spur us to action. Without ambition, we are left to lament what might have been if only we had not been so casual. As we know, achievement depends on our competence and ranges from the noble and noteworthy to venal and despicable. What we value and believe at the center of our being influences—*causes*—our ambition to lead us to strivings that are more or less noble and noteworthy. For instance, we may selfishly serve our own needs without worrying about the effects of our actions on colleagues. In fact, we may do this out of a conscious and deliberate disregard of values that place the welfare of colleagues equal to or above our own.

Tendencies to behave in this way clearly are conditioned by how our values and beliefs influence, mediate, and govern our choices and behaviors; that is, how our *conscience* comes into play in our lives. If our values and beliefs teach us that self-preservation and self-promotion are to be pursued ahead of the happiness and welfare of others, then we'll be likely to be comfortable with actions that support our priority on self-interest. In deciding whether that's something we should celebrate, it may help to think about people whose consciences allow them to be egoistic self-promoters and compare them with people who are more other-oriented.

What attributes do you associate with self-promoters? Do you think of them as cool, smart, rational, and wise, or do you regard them as selfish, narcissistic, self-serving, and insensitive? What comes to mind when you think of people who are more other-oriented? Do they tend to be labeled wise or foolish; caring or insensitive; kind or callous; generous or selfish? Which labels, in values terms, are to be preferred in light of the importance of general welfare? More specifically, which kinds of labels would you, in your particular school setting, prefer to have associated with your behavior?

When I think of someone who's self-promoting, I think of someone who's

Realistic	1	2	3	4	5	Idealistic
Selfish	1	2	3	4	5	Generous
Warm	1	2	3	4	5	Aloof
Pitiable	1	2	3	4	5	Admirable

Our preferences in this matter are probably transparent to a fault. We prefer to think, of course, that generosity of spirit, philanthropy, and concern for others are usually—not always, of course, but usually—*better for* everyone and therefore to be preferred to selfishness, self-promotion, and indifference toward the needs of others.

What would *you* prefer to be known for? More importantly, perhaps, we should ask what it would be *better for* you to be known for, and what would it be better for *others* for you to be known for? Will human welfare be affected in preferable ways according to the choices our values and beliefs lead us to make? Will the human condition be influenced more positively by values and beliefs that incline us toward benign behavior rather than malignant? Are beliefs that nurture traitors comparable to those that create teachers? Should principals care whether their students aspire to become poets, punks, prostitutes, or priests? Should principals care whether the effects of their values and beliefs cause their students to think indolence and industry are equivalent, or that sloppy effort is indistinguishable from careful work?

Make no mistake about it. There is a normative value/preference at work here, which hopes you will be more saint than sinner. We are urging a point of view on you that an "objective scholar" might be reluctant to recommend on the grounds that objectivity requires neutrality of position, and that neutrality precludes imposing preferences on others. We might agree in part, on the ground that principles of liberty require us to respect your freedom to choose, but we also probably would go a step farther and argue that where a value such as general welfare is concerned, there is really no justifiable values basis for arguing against it. When the choice is between an ideal of the sort embodied in a term such as "general welfare" or "equal opportunity" and one such as "competitive advantage," there is really nothing to argue about.

Some will vigorously object, protesting that competition is what made America great. You may hear this preference supported by views holding, for instance, that the most fit of any species are the ones who not only survive, but the ones who *deserve* to survive; that "might *makes* right," or, as the operative term "makes" connotes, power is the thing, phenomenon, or attribute that determines appropriateness of policy, principle, and action.

We hope, however, that you are aware that varied values perspectives can be and are brought into play by picking among alternative choices, and that you are persuaded that giving certain values greater weight in choices does have enormous influence on the near, intermediate, and long-term consequences of choice. Along with this critical understanding, we hope that you can detect inconsistencies in positions and arguments that are associated with inconsistencies and contradictions in values and beliefs.

Remember the earlier discussion (Chapter 2) about the critical roles played by *all*, *some*, and *none* in our construction of logical arguments. Recall that it is possible to argue, for instance, that *all* competition, *some* competition, or *no* competition is a good thing. Also remember that *context* is an important thing to consider when attempting to evaluate the goodness of an argument. Following this format, we might argue that in *all* (the qualifying term) competitions between *good* and *evil* individuals or entities (the contextual attribute), it is preferable for the good individual or entity to prevail.

You will also recognize, of course, that contextual attributes change. Competitions are not always between individuals or entities that are clearly distinguishable as to their meritorious attributes and conduct. Not only is it not always easy to judge the merits of people and organizations, but people and organizations sometimes take measures deliberately intended to deceive observers with regard to the goodness of their intentions and to the appropriateness of the means employed in pursuit of those intentions or ends. We have heard reports, for example, of school districts whose employees deliberately, as a matter of unwritten policy, avoid giving full information to the parents of children with handicaps in order to avoid incurring costs for evaluations and provision of services. Law in this case substantially prescribes the "end." Aside from the probable illegality of the practice, what does the alleged behavior imply about the ethics of educators who would employ it?

The important point to us, though, is that value-laden debates are *precisely* the things that rancorously divide contemporary cultures. To illustrate, let us consider again the example provided by world religions, which shall for purposes of discussion be designated A, B, and C. We need to know nothing for the sake of discussion save that each of these religions is regarded by its adherents as "the one, true faith." If we place much stock in definitions, we will soon recognize that "one, true faith" does not admit the possibility of there being two or three. One is a very concise number. If each of three faiths, then, claim to be "the one...," and if each of the three also refuses to enter into any sort of discussion to establish peaceful understanding and/or coexistence, it doesn't take much of an intellectual leap to understand that a serious problem exists. It is ironic, is it not, to think that faith—a values position, to be sure—can be of such paradoxical nature that it can both require us to love everyone, enemies included, and (by the way) kill them if they either deny the legitimacy of our faith or refuse to accept it.

What if anything is to be done in this sort of situation? One possible approach involves asking holders of conflicting values positions whether there is any value or good that is sufficiently greater than the one at the root of the disagreement to convince the disputants to strike a compromise. (see Fisher, Ury, & Patton, 1991, for possible strategies). In other words, is your commitment to the notion that *your* faith is the "one, true..." so compelling that you would make the ultimate sacrifice in its behalf, or is it possible to think that life itself is so precious that disagreement over possibly moot issues of religious supremacy should be subordinate to it?

If assertions about inviolability of certain values are held to be absolutely true, and if one such assertion is in obvious conflict with another, the salient outcome is fairly transparent: rancorous conflict or some sort of war. The central question for all parties in these circumstances is the same: Am I willing to entertain a compromise on closely held values? If the answer is no, and if dignified withdrawal is not a possibility, then the parties wield power to determine whether *their* "truth" shall prevail.

As we write this, we also think about the probability that the depth and complexity of issues involved will frustrate you. You've noted that we hold certain values to be superior to, or more desirable than others. In other words, not all values are relative. Some are, of course, but not all. You also may have noted that values sometimes have a frustrating capacity to "change their spots"—to decline or be displaced by some other value according to a shift in context. Some would characterize this by saying "the stakes went up" or "so-and-so upped the ante." That happens.

In the example from world religions, an influential leader may have a revelation that demands that life be recognized as more precious than sectarian dominance. Coreligionists who were not privileged to share the vision do not always treat this sort of revelatory experience with respect. The prophet, in fact, may be viewed as a traitor by more prosaic, but still interested players—interested, perhaps, to such a great extent that their "interests" would warrant rewarding the visionary's courage with martyrdom.

These are the sorts of issues that presently rend the social and cultural fabric of America and the world. They set privileged against deprived, rich against poor, and advantaged against disadvantaged. As you think about yourself, we hope you will reflect on the influences you will wield in your school. What kind of place will you strive to make it? Would you have it be the kind of place where the privileged have only to nod to have their wishes granted, while the underprivileged must grovel—and show extraordinary promise—to receive what the advantaged take as a matter-of-fact? From a perspective which is probably challenging—perhaps to a degree that is unhelpful—we would encourage you to reflect on whether an *educator*—one who deserves the title—should pander to the whims of the elite while ignoring the groans, however silent, of the deprived.

You have ambition, competence, and conscience. Everyone who reads these words will, of necessity, have different amounts and kinds of each; every reader also will find ambition, competence, and conscience tempered by values and beliefs that differ.

SEARCHING FOR INCONGRUENCIES

In taking up consideration of how one minimizes or eliminates incongruous attributes or elements that may occasionally intrude on and disrupt harmonies that should be apparent among thoughts, words, and actions, we might put a helpful beginning to it by examining the meaning of the key term. *Incongruous,* according to *Webster's Comprehensive Dictionary, 2nd ed.* (1996, p. 640), is synonymous with

> absurd, conflicting, contradictory, contrary, discordant, discrepant, ill-matched, inapposite, inappropriate, incommensurable, incompatible, inconsistent, inharmonious, irreconcilable, mismatched, mismated, repugnant, unsuitable. Two or more things that do not fit well together, or are not adapted to each other....

You might want to begin your deliberations on how to go about achieving consistency and noncontradiction among values, beliefs, and behaviors by concentrating on the meaning conveyed by the synonyms listed above for *incongruous.* What intent do they convey? Taken together, do they bring an image to mind that is positive, exemplary, and desirable—an image that you hope others associate with your leadership style? Or do they tend more to build up an image you would rather not have associated with your persona—either as principal or citizen? The questions themselves signify an implicit values preference —one which favors consistency.

But we digress. Let us return to the question: How do we search for, and then effectively harmonize, or remove, incompatible, disturbing, disruptive inconsistencies? The quest obviously must begin with a successful assault on a logical impossibility—to become knowledgeable about what we cannot know. *Can* we know what we can*not* know? Logically, we can't. But if we back off a step and ask whether it is *possible* to *know* what we *do not* know, the possibilities become more encouraging. We have compelling reasons to believe we can learn, for example. Learning entails becoming knowledgeable about or skilled at what we currently do not know or cannot do. The proven possibility of learning justifies both our faith and our efforts.

Having said this, what are some issues to be concerned about and obstacles to be overcome in our quest for consistency? One starting point that is certain to be beneficial is self-awareness. To whatever extent you may presently behave in reflexive, unreflective ways, you probably will be both unaware of and uninterested in how your behaviors complement each other and your values and beliefs. A productive starting point, then, might consist of a brief self-inventory of the following kinds of questions.

The questions in Figure 5.3 convey certain values positions: You *should* be concerned about how others view your behavior. The information you have in that regard *should* be accurate. You also *should* recognize that the information has to be used if it is to be of benefit. The last three questions move from others' views to your own. Question 4 demands self-scrutiny and sometimes-brutal honesty if it is to yield benefits. You cannot hope to achieve a unified wholeness among thoughts, words, and deeds if you lie to yourself about how congruent these elements are. Similarly, it is important that the bases of your knowledge be valid, and that your interest in being well and accurately informed be genuine.

Once your self-awareness and self-interest begin to develop, you may then begin more systematically to address incongruous features you identify among your values, beliefs, and actions. At a foundational level, you will need to ask whether your values are congruent or in harmony with what are known to be

---

FIGURE 5.3. BRIEF SURVEY ON SELF-AWARENESS

---

1. How concerned am I about others' perceptions of my behavior?

   Not at all • • • • • • *Very much*

2. How accurate is my understanding of others' perceptions?

   Totally • • • • . • • *Zero*

3. How highly do I value this sort of information?

   Invaluable • • • • • • *Worthless*

4. How accurate is my own information about my behavior?

   No clue • • • • • . • *Totally*

5. How do I know?

   Evidence • • • • • • *I don't*

6. How committed am I to becoming accurately informed?

   Not very • • • • • • *Highly*

---

in keeping with desirable, defensible aims or ends. We can suggest certain things here that we have come to hold to as primary values, but you really need to make your own lists, reflect on them, prioritize them, settle on some as being more primary, and then—as an additional, imperative step—think about how those may change with the passage of time and in the face of changing conditions.

WHAT DO YOU VALUE?

As you begin this exercise, you may find it productive to concentrate first on the professional side of your being. That is not to suggest that values that guide your professional and personal existence can be too disparate and remain defensibly consistent. It is to say, rather, that what you may share with others in a principalship preparation program or conversations with colleagues might be more beneficially undertaken if the focus is concentrated on principals' values, beliefs, and actions. You might begin with the list in Figure 5.4.

**FIGURE 5.4. AN ALPHABETICAL LISTING
OF ILLUSTRATIVE EDUCATIONAL VALUES**

Analytic skill	Education	Learning for learning's sake
Athletics	Equality of opportunity	Loyalty
Authentic assessment	Equity	Liberal education
Basic education	Factual knowledge	Mathematics
Clubs	Fairness	Personal competence
Collaboration	Fine and performing arts	Privilege according to status
Competitiveness	Flexibility	Problem solving
Compliant behavior	High achievement	Research-based practice
Consistency	High stakes tests	Rigorous standards
Cooperation	Honesty	School safety
Courtesy	Humanities	Science
Creation science	Humor	Schooling for work
Creativity	Inclusion	Standards
Critical thinking	Innovative teaching	Strict discipline
Data-driven practice	Integrity	Teacher competence
Dependability	Justice	Theory of evolution
Discipline	Languages	

It may be helpful to contemplate a couple of things as you review this list. First, is there one term that rises and shines above all the others as a primary educational value for you? What is it?

Think about it within the context of all the other terms. Having done so, do you think you could defend your choice in a serious debate? What if you picked "science"? Would someone who picked "education" be more strongly positioned to argue that her choice is more fundamental than yours? What about "Learning for learning's sake" versus "Schooling for work"? Is a society or a culture that organizes its schools on the fundamental principle of providing employees for business and industry better or worse off than the society that pegs its fortunes to the notion that knowledge—general knowledge, in and of itself—is a more basic or higher value than preparing compliant workers for a sometimes fickle and unpredictable marketplace?

"Education should be research-based and data-driven." How many times have you heard that? What intention does it convey? That is, what does it mean? While the phrase has become almost a mantra within practitioners' circles, it probably should still be subject to careful scrutiny regarding its deeper meanings and implications for other, perhaps more humanitarian, concerns that may be implicated. If we take the assertions of practitioners who have heard and come to appreciate the mantra as an example, we may also have seized upon a group who are indisputably well meaning, but inadequately informed. For example, what if wee Johnny, the poor, abused second grader with learning disabilities, cannot read? (You will recall, of course, the many outraged allusions to "Why Johnny can't....") How does wee Johnny "fit," in the overall scheme of "research-based" and "data-driven"? Just where, pray, does an *individual* come into the equation? More critical, perhaps, is the question: "Where *should* the individual come into play?" Research and data—in the hands of a zealot—can become crude and ineffective instruments. If "data" includes insightful observations of Johnny's learning impediments by skilled, conscientious teachers, then it may deserve an elevated status as an educational value. If it tends to be confined to measured performance on high-stakes assessments, however, its ranking as a value should be reevaluated and moderated.

All of these are values issues. We have barely begun to scratch the surface with you. As you peruse the list you will see terms that almost seem to be fighting words, for example, creation science versus the theory of evolution. Where does your belief system take you on this? Does it demand adherence to some particular sectarian view? Does it demand that you genuflect before the objective throne of "science"—despite Einstein's assertion that science is nothing more than a particular form of bias? Does it consider possible differences between secular and sacred methods of time keeping? In short, does it take careful account of the differences between *objective* and *subjective* evidence? What do you make of it? Should "creation science" hold sway on your list, or should "education"? Which of these two, in all seriousness, is buttressed by an array of supporting information sufficient to convince us that it should hold sway over the other in a ranking of values? Does God *really* make time appear to "stand still" (see Strike, Haller, & Soltis, 1998) so as to confuse our minds with regard to "evolution," or should we rather…? Is there believable evidence that bears on the issue? What does the evidence suggest? Are there features or attributes of the evidence that should give us pause? What are they?

How do we distinguish between compelling evidence and superstition? Where is the line of demarcation separating fact from fiction—saga from myth? What sort of evidence is required to justify standing before a patriarch of our clan and claiming that the cultural lore handed down from generation to generation is sheer myth?

Our questions *may* be rhetorical (Golden, Berquist, & Coleman, 1992). And, again, they may not. In either case, how would you formulate an answer—either a private one to yourself, as permitted by rhetorical queries, or an *actual* answer—in case the question is real? How *would* you answer? Really?

Would you say education is most important? Learning for learning's sake? Preparation for work? Has it occurred to you to think that an unsafe school is no school at all? Where *are* you on these issues? Do you really agree at your most fundamental level with the postmodernists, that everything is relative? We sincerely hope you do not.

What do you think about these issues? *Do* alternative values differ, or are they all—in the final analysis—relative? Does it make any difference what we value—*really?* Does it make any difference what we believe—*really?* Does it make any difference how we act—*really?* We urge you to keep one thing firmly in mind: If it truly made no difference—*really*—what we valued, believed, and did, then, as we have already suggested, any consideration of why values *count* would be absurd.

A POSSIBLE ROAD TO CLARITY

As you take steps to compare alternative educational values and bring defensible order to them, you might find it helpful to do the following exercise. First, review the alphabetical listing of values and delete any that you can logically and persuasively demonstrate as inappropriate for inclusion in your personal system of values and beliefs. Second, add any missing values terms required to make the listing acceptably complete for you. Third, prioritize the list, using a system that orders the terms from most central, core, or important, to least so. This step should be taken in a way that allows for ties.

Fourth, pick two or three pairs of values that would probably be perceived by observers to be in conflict if you did not handle them appropriately. Constancy (or integrity) and flexibility would be one. Basic education and liberal education *might* be another. Learning for learning's sake and schooling for work would compose a third pair.

As you formulate your positions on and arguments for those positions regarding how you will deal with potentially contradictory values, you might want to begin by evaluating each pair with regard to whether they are in an *either-or* relationship, or a *both-and* relationship with each other. For example, is it possible to *both* support learning for learning's sake *and* schooling for work without contradicting yourself? You might begin formulating your position on this particular pair by asking whether it is *necessarily* true that one *must* embrace *either* one *or* the other of these values. Would it be possible, for instance, to hold that it is acceptable to think learners should value knowledge for its own sake *and* be sensitive to the occupational implications of things studied? Work your positions and supporting arguments out individually at first.

As an extended culminating activity, plan four or more hours of exercises to include the following examples:

1. Describe and defend your most basic values and beliefs in teams. In the process, begin with those you would refuse to compromise, move through those that would clearly be paradoxical, and end with "negotiable" values (see Figure 5.2, p. 104). Take time to explain how you would act in avoiding either the fact or appearance of inconsistency and self-contradiction. Your description and defense, of course, should be constructed to clearly reflect their relationship to the ends you would intend them to serve.

2. Blend the teams back into a full group consideration of *examples* of values that were especially persuasive in terms of content, presentation, argument, and potential to exert beneficial influence which team members heard from their teammates. Take special pains to get at the *why* issues involved, as in: "Why would this be such a useful thing to be put into practice?"

3. Collect and document anecdotes from experience that illustrate positive and negative examples of consistent administrative behavior. Share them, either in written form or orally. Analyze them to specify and understand behaviors that signify consistency and others that consistently belie it.

4. Develop some role plays to be acted out before the group which challenge the person playing the role of principal to deny some espoused value or to otherwise act in ways that are incongruous. An example might involve an "attorney" asking a principal whether another principal's behavior in handling a student discipline case was competent. If the "principal" espouses loyalty to colleagues as a core value and also holds that loyalty to profession is central,

how does he or she respond when asked about behavior that is clearly incompetent—mistaking medical shock subsequent to a student's beating for substance abuse, for instance.

WHERE DO WE LEAVE THE CONVERSATION (AND VICE VERSA)?

As the section heading implies, it seems to be time to seek a satisfactory—and, if possible, satisfying—conclusion to our consideration of values and beliefs. However, as the *vice versa* suggests, the conversation on cultural values and philosophical beliefs is one that has multiple capacities for "leaving us" in a mind-boggling variety of states.

We hope that your experiences with the ideas, exercises, and attempts to persuade included in these pages have left you better informed and more settled about what you believe than when you started. We also hope that you might agree that conversations about values and beliefs are properly viewed as things that we really should *not* leave. This bit of encouragement to think of values and beliefs having sufficient instrumental and imperative value or worth themselves to deserve our regular, systematic, thoughtful attention is itself the product of values and beliefs that we hold in high regard. They have taught us that people who engage regularly and productively in examining and adjusting their values and beliefs are, in the final analysis, people who come closest to achieving the ideals of democracy. This is particularly true of assistant principals and principals who are particularly adept at servant leadership.

Do not take encouragement to engage regularly in examining your values and beliefs as license to become indecisive and ambivalent about *where* you stand and what you stand *for*. It is, rather, encouragement to be vigilant that what you stand for is consistent with the ideals of democratic existence—existence characterized by concern for general welfare, equality of opportunity, safety, the pursuit of happiness, and processes which are of, by, and for "the people."

Where should the conversation "leave" us, given its many capacities? Our hope would be that it would leave you strongly committed to the idea that democracy is both a value and belief that deserves prominent emphasis in schools. We also hope that the conversation leaves you optimistic about the possibilities of schools that are more democratically organized, and feeling energetically competent to lead your schools to a realization of democratic ideals in their organization and operation.

ACTION FOLLOW-UP

If you already are a principal or assistant principal, you probably will be able to rely on personal experience to complete these exercises. If you are a teacher, you also probably have had experiences upon which you can rely to complete the exercises. After reading them, if you feel that you have not directly experienced anything of the sort implied, you should consult with two or three principals, asking them to describe two or three of the most difficult, threatening dilemmas they've ever faced. In any event, be mindful of the need to respect professional confidences and to avoid disclosing information or identities that would constitute unprofessional or unlawful invasions of privacy.

- ◆ Describe two or three moral dilemmas or crises of conscience you've experienced in your role as an educational leader.

- ◆ Did the experiences have anything in common; that is, were you expected to say or do things which were in strong, direct conflict with your central values and beliefs or your sense of who you are? Describe them.

- ◆ Were you able to address the dilemmas in ways that allowed you to preserve your personal identity, integrity, and conscience? If yes, what specific behaviors supported the accomplishment. If no, have you subsequently been able to recover the losses incurred in the experience or to compensate for them in helpful ways? If you have, describe how that became possible. If you have not, comment on any possibilities that occur to you as you reflect on the matter.

♦ With a partner, perhaps the same one(s) you worked with in the exercises from chapters one and two,
specify *the range of consequences* that can result from
inconsistencies in principals' values and beliefs. Focus your attention and efforts on undesirable/nega-
tive consequences of inconsistency and describe
promising steps you will take to achieve and maintain congruence or consistency between and among
your values and beliefs. Comment briefly on the
probable, observable effects on your school of your
success in this endeavor.

REFERENCES

The American Heritage Dictionary, 2nd ed. 1985. Boston: Houghton Mifflin.

Aristotle. 1952 (orig. ca 350 BCE). *Nichomachean Ethics.* In *The Great Books,* no. 9, Aristotle II, trans., W.D. Ross. Chicago: Encyclopaedia Britannica.

Bass, B. M. 1990. *Bass & Stogdill's Handbook of Leadership, 3rd ed.* New York: The Free Press.

Beck, L. G., and J. Murphy. 1994. *Ethics in Educational Leadership Programs: An Expanding Role.* Thousand Oaks, CA: Corwin Press.

Berliner, D., and B. Biddle. 1995. *The Manufactured Crisis: Myths, Fraud, and the Attack on America's Public Schools.* Reading, MA: Addison-Wesley.

Berliner, D. C., 1997. "Educational Psychology Meets the Christian Right: Differing Views of Children, Schooling, Teaching and Learning." *Teachers College Record.* 98, 3 (Spring): 382–415.

Berkeley, G. 1952 (Originally about 1710). "A Treatise Concerning the Principles of Human Knowledge." In *Great Books of the Western World, Vol. 35.* Chicago: Encyclopaedia Britannica.

Bertocci, P. A. 1980. "Personalistic Philosophy of Education." In *Education and Values,* ed. D. Sloan. New York: Teachers College Press.

Boorstin, D. 1961. *The Image: A Guide to Pseudo-Events in America.* New York: Harper and Row.

Bruner, J., J. J. Goodnow, and G. A. Austin. 1967. *A Study of Thinking.* New York: Science Editions. Cited in *Models of Teaching, 3rd Ed.,* by B. Joyce and M. Weil. 1986. Englewood Cliffs, NJ: Prentice-Hall.

Burns, J.M. 1978. *Leadership.* New York: Harper and Row.

Carlson, R.V. 1996. *Reframing and Reform: Perspectives on Organization, Leadership, and School Change.* White Plains, NY: Longman Publishers.

Carroll, L. 1977. *Symbolic Logic.* Ed., W.W. Bartley, III. New York: Clarkson N. Potter.

Collins, J. C., and J. I. Porras. 1997. *Built to Last: Successful Habits of Visionary Companies.* New York: HarperCollins.

Csikszentmihalyi, M. 1997. *Finding Flow.* New York: Basic Books.

Deal, T. E., and K. D. Peterson. 1994. *The Leadership Paradox: Balancing Logic and Artistry in Schools.* San Francisco: Jossey-Bass.

deJouvenel, B. 1967. *The Art of Conjecture.* New York: Basic Books.

Deming, W. E. 1994. *The New Economics for Industry, Government, Education, 2nd Ed.* Cambridge, MA: Massachusetts Institute of Technology.

Dewey, J. 1910. *Scientific Philosophy.* Quoted in *The Enduring Questions: Main Problems of Philosophy, 5th Ed.,* by M. Rader and J. H. Gill. 1991. Orlando, FL: Holt, Rinehart and Winston.

Fischer, L. D. Schimmel, and C. Kelly. 1999. *Teachers and the Law, 5th Ed.* New York: Longman.

Fisher, R., W. Ury, and B. Patton. 1991. *Getting to Yes: Negotiating Agreement without Giving In, 2nd Ed.* New York: Penguin Books.

Gardner, J. 1961. *Excellence: Can We Be Equal and Excellent Too?* New York: Harper and Row.

Golden, J. L., G. F. Berquist, and W. E. Coleman. 1992. *The Rhetoric of Western Thought 5th Ed.* Dubuque, IA: Kendall-Hunt.

Gutmann, A. 1987. *Democratic Education.* Princeton: Princeton University Press.

Hellerstein, N. 1985. "Diamond: A Logic of Paradoxes." *Cybernetics* 1, 101–14.

Hoy, W. K., and C. G. Miskel. 1987. *Educational Administration: Theory, Research and Practice, 3rd Ed.* New York: Random House.

Interstate School Leaders Licensure Consortium. 1996. *Standards for School Leaders.* Washington, DC: Council of Chief State School Officers.

Jefferson, T. 1776. *The Declaration of Independence.* Version cited published by the Kansas Secretary of State. Topeka: October, 1995.

Joyce, B., and M. Weil. 1986. *Models of Teaching, 3rd Ed.* Englewood Cliffs, NJ: Prentice-Hall.

Kant, I. 1959. *Foundations for the Metaphysics of Morals.* Trans. L.W. Beck. New York: Bobbs-Merrill. Quoted in Sergiovanni, 1992, *Infra.* Originally published 1785.

Kidder, R.M. 1994. *Shared Values for a Troubled World: Conversations with Men and Women about Conscience.* San Francisco: Jossey-Bass.

Kohlberg, L. 1983. *Moral Stages: A Current Formulation and Reply to Critics.* Basel: S. Karger.

Kohn, A. 1993. *Punished by Rewards: The Trouble with Gold Stars, Incentive Plans, A's, Praise, and Other Bribes.* New York: Houghton Mifflin.

Kouzes, J. M., and B. Z. Posner. 1993. *Credibility: How Leaders Gain and Lose it, Why People Demand It.* San Francisco: Jossey-Bass.

Leiser, B. M. 1973. *Liberty, Justice and Morals: Contemporary Value Conflicts.* New York: MacMillan.

McQuarrie, F. O., Jr. 1991. "The Imperatives of Ownership, Commitment and Trust." In *The Moral Imperatives of Leadership: A Focus on Human Decency,* ed. B. G. Barnett, F. O. McQuarrie, and C. J. Norris. Memphis, TN: National Policy Board for Educational Administration.

Mill, J. S. 1859.*On Liberty.* Quoted in *The Enduring Questions: Main Problems of Philosophy, 5th Ed.,* by M. Rader and J. H. Gill. 1991. Orlando, FL: Holt, Rinehart and Winston.

National Association of Elementary School Principals. 1976. *Statement of Ethics for School Administrators.* Available at: http://www.naesp.org/ethics.htm

National Education Goals Panel. 1994. *The National Education Goals Report. Building a Nation of Learners.* Washington, DC: U.S. Government Printing Office.

The New International Webster's Comprehensive Dictionary of the English Language. 1996. Naples, FL: Trident Press International.

Peters, R. S. 1980. "Democratic Values and Educational Aims." In *Education and Values,* by D. Sloan. 1980. New York: Teachers College Press.

Phillips, D.T. 1992. *Lincoln on Leadership: Executive Strategies for Tough Times.* New York: Warner Books.

Pinker, S. 1997. *How the Mind Works.* New York: W.W. Norton.

Postman, N. 1985. *Amusing Ourselves to Death: Public Discourse in the Age of Show Business.* New York: Viking Penguin.

Rawls, J. 1971. *A Theory of Justice.* Cambridge, MA: Harvard University Press.

Reed, E. S. 1996. "Selves, Values, Cultures." In *Values and knowledge,* eds. E.S. Reed, E. Turiel, and T. Brown. Mahwah, NJ: Lawrence Erlbaum.

Roe v. Wade, 410 U.S. 113 (1973).

Roszak, T. 1994. *The Cult of Information: A Neo-Luddite Treatise on High-Tech, Artificial Intelligence, and the True art of Thinking.* Berkeley, CA: University of California Press.

Sergiovanni, T. J. 1992. *Moral Leadership: Getting to the Heart of School Improvement.* San Francisco: Jossey-Bass.

Sergiovanni, T. J. 1995. *The Principalship: A Reflective Practice Perspective.* Needham Heights, MA: Allyn and Bacon.

Shaw, W.H. 1993. *Social and Personal Ethics.* Belmont, CA: Wadsworth.

Simon, H.A. 1957. *Administrative Behavior, 2nd Ed.* New York: The Free Press.

Spring, J.H. 1997. *Conflict of Interests: The Politics of American Education, 3rd Ed.* New York: McGraw-Hill.

St. Thomas Aquinas. *Summa Theologiae.* (1966 ed., orig. 1485). Great Britain: Eyre and Spottiswoode.

Strike, K. A., E. J. Haller, and J. F. Soltis. 1988. *The Ethics of School Administration, 2nd Ed.* New York: Teachers College Press.